The Grey Wolfe Storybook

An Anthology
Supporting Michigan's
Special Needs Children
2014

Edited by Lisa M. Wolfe

Grey Wolfe Publishing, LLC
PO Box 1088
Birmingham, Michigan 48009
www.GreyWolfePublishing.com

© 2014 Grey Wolfe Publishing, LLC
Published by Grey Wolfe Publishing, LLC
www.GreyWolfePublishing.com
All Rights Reserved

ISBN: 978-1628280456
Library of Congress Control Number: 2014915007

The Grey Wolfe Storybook 2014

Edited by Lisa M. Wolfe

Dedication

We humbly dedicate this book to the special children of Michigan. These boys and girls play, compete, and learn with a unique perspective on the world; and we celebrate their unfailing strength and unbridled joy.

We also want to dedicate this book to the grandparents, parents, siblings, extended family and friends who give of themselves, tirelessly, day in and day out, to love Michigan's special children with unconditional acceptance and support.

Hello and Welcome to our Storybook!

Open your mind to a peak behind-the-curtains into the homes and lives of extraordinary characters. You may identify with children who are building forts and playing games, or with others who enjoy each day as if it's their last.

Expect to laugh and cry as these stories touch your heart. Learn life lessons such as what it's like to have a *Little Cup* and how the smallest act of kindness makes a big impact.

Thank you for your support. The proceeds benefit Michigan's special needs children.

A big thank you to our authors for sharing these memories with us.

Enjoy, and let me be the first to welcome you home.

~ Lisa M. Wolfe; Editor

Welcome Home
Lisa M. Wolfe

Welcome home
Where roads connect
To eyes that hold you
Thoughts and words
For you alone

Welcome home
Where doors unlock
With smells to greet you
Chairs to seat you
Intellect and emotions cemented in stone

Welcome home
Where sidewalks end
At grass to lay you
Trees to climb you
Intuition and wisdom
Merge as one

Welcome home
Where walls can speak
Of stories about you
Pictures contain you
Love and comfort
Forever overgrown

Contents

1.
A Badly Scuffed Baseball
J. J. Steinfeld

There is, near the end, I hope
a moment that is somehow ironic
and so side-splittingly humorous
that for that moment
you forget that you are at the end
little time to sum up, to start a new prayer
to get an old prayer exact
word for word
and then, for an instant,
guilt that is both ironic and humorous
you recall, at last, where you misplaced
love and imagination and a badly scuffed baseball
that you, at ten or thereabouts,
used to communicate
with the past and the future
against a brick wall near your house
a house that saw other endings
now your ending
your desire for irony and humour
for one last throw
against a brick wall
that almost revealed everything
to a child who threw and threw
a baseball until it was scuffed
like the clouds of heaven

2.

A Ghost In Powder Hollow
William Doreski

We'd smoked half the pack of Luckies Jerry had stolen from the supermarket. Outside, the summer air smelled of pine and hickory, but in the hideout the smoke hung in a greasy haze. "Hey. Geez. What's that?" Brian peered from the scrap lumber doorway.

Jerry and I crouched beside him and stared into the woods. Light and leaf-shade quivered in the hot August breeze. I didn't exactly see, but I vaguely sensed something watching us. "What is it?" I asked Brian.

"Something's watching us. I saw it. Something creepy." Jerry and I crawled out of the dugout. "Hey you!" Jerry shouted. Nothing but the breeze stirred. Yet something was really there. We all knew it. We crawled back inside. We had just discovered this odd structure, half above, half under the ground, a rain shelter built by older kids to conceal and focus their rebellion. A litter of Boy's Life magazines covered the dirt floor. Cigarette burn-holes scarred the pages, and three empty beer cans, crushed against some bony forehead, lounged in a corner. Jerry's older brother probably belonged to the gang of high-school punks that had dug this shallow hole and boarded it over, but Jerry knew better than to tell him we'd found his hideaway.

"Hey, some creep's out there. Creep! Pervert! Peeping Tom!" I yelled through the doorway without showing my face. But we knew that what was watching us wasn't any creep, wasn't some tough high school kid, wasn't a deer or bear. It was a ghost. That winter, when snow lay deep in the woods, I walked my dog every afternoon after school. The river had frozen over. Lady and I followed its rough undulations for miles, avoiding the few black open holes where fast current raced along. The river was shallow, usually no more than two feet deep, so there was little danger. One gloomy afternoon with snowflakes adrift in the iron cold, Lady and I left the river and climbed the bluff. I wanted to see what the dugout looked like with snow on it.

The woods looked unfamiliar in winter, and I had trouble finding the dugout. Snow had poured into the opening and filled the interior, until there was no longer a shelter, but something like a tomb. As I stood there, I felt the presence creep over me. It was out there watching. Lady, my beagle-spaniel mix, growled. Lady rarely growled, but she didn't like whatever was watching us in that snowy landscape, the hemlocks bent to the ground, the leafless hardwoods lean and purple-gray in the woolen light.

"What is it, girl?" I peered into the trees and right in her sight line saw a quiver of shadow half hidden by a hemlock bough. When I'd been with the other kids I hadn't felt even a shiver of fear, but now the chill came over me, and I dashed through the knee-deep snow with Lady struggling along beside me. I picked her up and we tumbled down the bluff in the soft cover and staggered out to the road. Lady wiggled with joy. She liked adventure, even if it was a little scary.

Not long ago I climbed the bluff to find the dugout I hadn't seen in forty years. There it was, right where we'd left it, the roof collapsed, the lumber rotted almost to oblivion, the magazines buried under a tangle of weeds. A sour reek of something dead rose from the mess. No one had used this shelter in a long, long time. I stood looking into the shallow hole, and then felt something watching me. For a moment, I hesitated. *Too old for this stuff.* But when I turned and caught a glimpse of the ghost, light and shade flickering, formless and poised, I was glad enough to believe in it again.

3.
Affection to Dye For
Terry Sanville

By mid-afternoon I reached the rickety barn-like building that Grandpop called "the factory". Thirsty from my hour-long walk in the August heat, I wrapped my mouth around a water faucet in the yard – the iron taste of it satisfying even though the water was warm and rusty.

Grandpop was inside at his machine making gold-handled brooms.

"Whatcha doin' Pop Pop?" I shouted the obvious.

"Got no time for ya, Tony. Got an order to fill," he yelled over the machine's racket.

"I'll go play with the cat," I hollered back. He smiled and waved me off.

Grandpop only worked until four, so I didn't have long to wait. Creeping toward a set of open wooden stairs, I passed Hawkins sitting in his office, filling out order forms. He looked up from his desk and frowned.

"Where da ya think you're going?" he demanded. His dark beard shadow looked like coffee grounds.

"Just ta the loft. I'll stay outta you way."

"Make sure you do," he ordered then returned to his paperwork.

I sprinted for the stairs and bounded upward to where the tangy-smelling broomcorn was stored and a flock of pigeons cooed in the rafters. I liked to go there and watch the machinery work on the open shop floor below. All the equipment to assemble the brooms was driven by an interconnected system of belts and pulleys powered by a tiny diesel engine that chuffed away in the yard. It was neat to follow the belt drive from its source. I watched it passed through various pulley wheels, changing directions all the while, and ended up connected to the machine that Grandpop stood at all day, sweat dripping off his bald head, his bent fingers attaching cut stalks of broomcorn to brightly colored wooden handles with thick silver wire.

The sun beat on the factory's metal roof, radiating heat directly inward. I sat near a glassless window on the edge of one of several dyeing tanks, my back to the wall, enjoying the Pacific breeze. An orange tabby cat with chewed-up ears and a white tipped tail trotted up and head-butted my legs, meowing loudly. I reached down and pulled him into my lap, his legs and claws extended. I could feel the rumble of his purring as I stroked his back and he gazed at me through half-closed eyes. I leaned back against the wall and looked up at the pigeons cooing. The hot afternoon stretched out before me, much like the cat in my lap. The rhythmic machine sounds lulled me to sleep.

"COME ON, IT'S TIME." I heard the shout from below. Startled and half awake, I quickly stumbled to my feet.

The machinery was turned off and the sun had dropped a couple of inches toward the horizon. I heard a splash and a loud meow. The tabby cat-paddled in the three-foot-deep vat. It tried to climb out, complaining, and using the worst possible language.

The tank was filled with brilliant, aniline dye to color the broomcorn and give it a green industrial look. I snatched at the cat with my right hand, going for the scruff of his neck. But I missed and my arm went under to the elbow. On my second try I hauled the tabby up and out, causing more caterwauling and hindquarter flicking that added green stripes to my T-shirt but fortunately missed my face.

I dropped the cat and it low-tailed it down the stairs, past Grandpop and Hawkins who were going over last-minute paperwork. They broke into raucous laughter as the green streak shot by. The tabby stopped in the yard to lick his coat, which just turned the cat's tongue an emerald shade.

"Oh Lord Almighty!" Hawkins exclaimed when he saw me clomp down the stairs. Both continued laughing. I thought they'd get sick.

Grandpop finally recovered. "Tony, that arm of yours is gonna stay green for a long, long time."

"Really? Neat-o-rama. Wait til I show Rudy and Jeeder."

"I'd worry more about your Mom and Dad," Grandpop said, chortling. He handed me a rag and I dried off as best I could. I was afraid the cat wouldn't forgive me for dumping him in the tank. But during the remainder of that summer, when I'd visit Grandpop, the tabby would come up and nuzzle my legs and demand affection, although never when I was near the dyeing vats.

Out in the yard, the ends of his fur caught the afternoon light and sparkled bright Kelly Green. I named him Kelly in honor of his dye job. By my next summer's vacation at Grandpop's he was almost normal color. By the summer after that he was gone.

4.
Aunt Aggie's Game
Melissa Grunow

Wearing Velcro shoes to school in the fourth grade is one of the worst decisions a kid could make, but Joey Dunbar didn't seem to realize he was doing anything wrong. Of the thirty kids in my class, Joey was the dumb one. All of us knew that he couldn't spell and he couldn't read very well, either. Even when he wrote his name, the letters looked loopy and smashed together like one of those swirly paintings that hung above the sink in the art room.

"Don't you know how to tie your shoes yet?" Derrick poked Joey in the shoulder and pointed at the shoes strapped to Joey's feet that he was trying to cover with playground gravel while he waited for the bell to ring.

Joey didn't say anything. He just stared at the ground, running the toe of his Velcro shoe back and forth through the dust and the rocks.

"Stupid!" Derrick smacked Joey in the back of the head, then ran away with his friends before any of the lunch aides noticed. He knew Joey wouldn't tell on him because he never did. Joey really couldn't do much about anything.

He couldn't even do math, which I didn't understand because math was so easy. Mrs. Rappaport told Mom that I was the best math student in the class. That's why I was able to work alone doing fractions while the rest of the class struggled through long division. Sometimes I was asked to help the students who didn't understand, but that always meant I had to help Joey. Sometimes I would pretend that I wasn't sure how to explain the problems to him so I wouldn't have to be near him. The worst thing that could happen to a person in my class was to be labeled as Joey's friend. There was no way I was going to let that happen to me.

There were other things wrong with Joey. He always wore corduroy pants and striped shirts with buttons and collars. He was sick all the time, too, so his nose looked crusty and he sniffled like a crybaby. To his face, most of the kids called him Crybaby Joey the Dumbhead. Behind his back, they said he was retarded. I didn't know what that meant, and Mom refused to tell me, so I settled on not talking to Joey. That way I knew I would never have to call him anything.

"Mom and Dad were fighting last night," my brother Isaac said with wide eyes and a serious face as we walked together from his first-grade class to the parking lot where Bumpa was waiting for us. I hated having to go to Isaac's class every day after school to get him because the first-graders smelled like pee.

I didn't say anything to him until after we were on the freeway heading toward Honey and Bumpa's cabin. We were sitting in the back of Bumpa's station wagon facing the car behind us. We called it the way back-back because it was behind the backseat; it was our favorite place to sit. We were going up north for the weekend while Mom and Dad stayed home to talk about "adult" things. They were always talking about "adult" things, and when they weren't talking, they were yelling at each other. At least, that's what Isaac said.

"Mom said Dad was a cheater, but they don't play games together anymore. I don't understand what game Mom was talking about." Isaac folded his arms and kicked the door. He was always kicking at stuff. Ever since Mom and Dad started their arguments, Isaac was mad all the time. He always heard them arguing because his room shared a wall with theirs. For a long time I didn't believe him, until one night they were yelling loud enough for me to hear, and they were throwing stuff. That was the night Mom broke the TV trying to throw a paperweight at Dad. It was the one Isaac got on a field trip to Greenfield Village and gave to her for Mother's Day.

"She didn't mean he cheats at games, dummy." I breathed on the window and drew hearts and stars on the glass. In the lane next to us I saw a girl who looked about my age. I waved, but she stuck out her tongue at me. I put my fingers in my mouth and pulled my lips apart, baring my teeth at her. I didn't feel very well. The spit in my mouth tasted hot, like Sour Patch Kids dipped in warm milk. I was going to have to try really hard not to throw up on this trip.

"Beth, do you think Mom and Dad hate each other now?" Isaac was a lot smarter at six than I had been, though I would never have told him that. Whenever there were any problems between Mom and Dad, Isaac had always known about them first.

"I don't know." I glanced over my shoulder, and my eyes met Bumpa's In the rearview mirror. "I don't want to think about it."

"Okay, kids. We're here," Bumpa said after he opened the tailgate for us to climb out. I looked out the window a little surprised. I rubbed my eyes and realized that I must have fallen asleep, which always happened when I rode in the car. Either I fell asleep, or I threw up. That's why Bumpa was always nervous about me riding in the way back-back; there was nowhere for the puke to go except all over the seat or all over Isaac.

"Hi, kids!" Our grandma waved at us from the other side of the screen door.

"Honey!" I pushed through the door and let it slam into the

back of Isaac's head. He kicked me, but I ignored him.

"Beth, you're getting so big! Did you get car sick on the way up here?"

I looked at the orange carpeting, my cheeks feeling warm. "No, Honey. I was okay."

"Puke-inator," Isaac whispered behind me and kicked my calf. "Grandma, did you make us the kiss cookies?" Isaac looked past her at the bare kitchen counter. The whole cabin smelled like sugar and melted fudge when it sticks to the bottom of the pan and the stirring bowl. I always offered to help Honey bake because she'd let me lick the spoon.

I scowled at Isaac for being rude, but I was wondering the same thing. I was the only one who referred to our grandma Honey. When I was a baby, Bumpa used to call her that all the time, and when I learned to talk, I started calling her Honey, too. The whole family thought it was so cute that they never let me just call her Grandma like Isaac did. I thought I was getting a little too old to be cute, but I didn't want to disappoint Honey.

The cabin looked exactly the same as it had the last time I visited. Everything was orange and chocolate brown and pea-green. It was always a lot warmer than our house and the chairs were so big and so old I felt like they were swallowing me whenever I sat in them.

Before Honey could answer about the cookies, Aunt Aggie came scurrying out of the back bedroom and plowed toward us with her arms wide open. She grabbed me by her shoulders and pulled me into her squishy body. Aunt Aggie was my favorite relative. She always played games with us while the other adults were too busy talking or doing chores. She still lived with Bumpa and Honey. She didn't have a husband or even a boyfriend, which was good because that meant she wasn't going to get married and have kids, then start ignoring me like my other two aunts.

"Hi, Aunt Aggie." My voice was muffled from her pushing my face into her soft and flabby chest. Sometimes Aunt Aggie's hugs were embarrassing because she would kiss my cheek a million times and swing me back and forth until I felt like throwing up.

"Beth Ann! How's my favorite niece?"

"Aunt Aggie!" I giggled at her and pressed my tongue between the gap in my teeth. "I'm your only niece."

"Agnes, would you let the kids get inside? They just got here." Honey had that rattle in her voice she always got when she was mad about something. It seemed like she was always mad at Aunt Aggie.

"Sorry." Aunt Aggie's smile was gone and her shoulders angled downward in such a way that her clothes looked like they were falling off a hanger that was too small. "Come on, Beth Ann," she said. "I'll help you put your stuff away."

****

"Isaac, let's watch something else." I tried to wrestle the remote controller from him, but he held on tight. My tummy was full from eating so many Spaghetti O's for dinner. I didn't really feel like watching T.V., but it was getting dark, so I couldn't play outside. I hated watching cartoons with Isaac because he always picked the stupid ones like "Night Rider" or "Batman and Robin," when I would have rather watched "My Little Pony" or "Rainbow Brite." Boy cartoons were stupid.

"No, I had the T.V. first, so I'm going to watch what I want to watch." Isaac pushed the remote between his legs and put a pillow over it, trying to block it from me. "You always get to pick what you want to watch, Beth. It's my turn."

"But I'm the oldest. Gimme the remote." I tried to push Isaac over, but it was as if he had chained himself to the floor in protest of girly cartoons. "You have to listen to me. I'm the oldest, so that means I'm the boss."

Isaac started kicking me and screaming, and I tried tickling and pinching him to get the remote. Why was he such a brat?

"No, I'm the boss." Honey was standing over us in her dish-washing apron, wiping suds off her arms with a pink hand towel. "Nobody's going to watch cartoon's because your grandpa will be coming in here in about ten minutes to watch T.V. You kids go play a game or something. Your young minds shouldn't rot away in front of cartoons. Play a game, then you both have to take a bath and go to bed."

I backed away from Isaac and decided to play with Aunt Aggie. If Mom would have told us to turn off the T.V. we would have argued and won, but we knew we couldn't do that with Honey. Honey always won. Isaac never even tried to throw a fit around Honey, because when Honey gave directions, she meant business.

I found Aunt Aggie in the laundry room folding towels. She only had one basket to do, but she was having a hard time getting the edges to line up so she had to refold almost all of them. Honey didn't like sloppy work, even from Aunt Aggie who never was really neat about anything, not even drawing or coloring.

"Hey, Aunt Aggie. Want some help?" I stood in the doorway. The strong bleach smell made me want to sneeze. Honey's laundry room always smelled like bleach and everything was white. Even the grooves in the tiles were white, as if she had picked every speck of dirt out with a toothpick. Honey always said, though, that you can't wash your clothes in a dirty room because then they won't come clean.

"If you want to. I'm almost done." Aunt Aggie smiled when she turned to look at me.

I picked up a towel and started folding. When she wasn't looking, I would refold one of her towels, so she wouldn't get yelled at. Sometimes I felt bad that she had to do all her chores two or three times because she couldn't get them right. "Do you want to play a game when we're done?"

"Sure, can we play Monopoly?" Aunt Aggie knew that Monopoly was my favorite game, so she made it hers, too. She began to pile the folded towels into the basket. "I just have to put these in the linen closet."

"I'll go set it up!" I went into the dining room, and carefully slid the box out from underneath the other boxes and off the shelf. I counted out the right amount of money for both Aunt Aggie and me, and set up the rest of the game. I even put our game pieces on "Go." Aunt Aggie was the Scotty dog. I was usually the car, but Honey's game was missing that piece, so I had to be the thimble. It didn't matter, though. I was just happy to play a game with Aunt Aggie without Isaac who was always bothering us. He always got mad whenever he lost, and I almost always won. The only time I lost was when Bumpa played, but usually he preferred to take naps.

Aunt Aggie finally came to the table to play. Within ten minutes she had landed herself in jail, and during every turn I had to count the money out for her and help her move the Scotty dog. Sometimes she couldn't read the names of the properties really well, or she didn't understand why they cost so much, and I would have to explain it to her. I always had to be the banker when the two of us played Monopoly because Aunt Aggie just couldn't count out the money. Her favorite part of the whole game was when she had to go to jail, so she tried as often as possible for her Scotty dog to sit on that corner of the board. She never tried to buy Boardwalk or Park Place, even if she landed on it before me. She knew that they were my two favorite properties, even though I always bought hotels, which usually made her lose the game. Every time we played Monopoly, Aunt Aggie didn't care if she won or lost. Often times, she didn't even know if she won or lost; she was just happy to be playing a game with her favorite niece, Beth Ann. Me.

"Hey, I wanna play, too!" Isaac climbed up onto one of the dining room chairs, and started sifting through the box for the wheelbarrow, his favorite piece.

"No, Isaac, we already started the game. Go do something else." I nudged his shoulder with mine while I rolled the dice. Double sixes. I loved rolling doubles because that meant that I got a second turn.

"You have to let me play, too. I don't have anything else to do." He put the wheelbarrow on "Go" and started digging the money out for himself. He didn't know how many of each bill he was supposed to get. He gave himself two twenties and ten ones.

"No, Isaac. Go away," Aunt Aggie said. "We already started the game. Besides, you always like to cheat, and nobody wants to play a game with a cheater."

Isaac looked at Aunt Aggie with nothing but anger in his face. I could tell he was thinking about the fight Mom and Dad had. "You big, fat dummy head!" Isaac flipped up one side of the game board so our pieces went all over the floor, then he kicked Aunt Aggie has hard as he could. I couldn't believe he did it. Aunt Aggie did act like a kid, but she was still a grown-up. Isaac would never kick Mom or Honey. It was just like the time he had to stand against the wall at recess because he had thrown his lunchbox at the wall and it gave some prissy girl a bloody nose. He almost got a detention, but Mom talked the principal out of it by telling him there were problems at home.

Aunt Aggie reached down and rubbed her calf, and when she looked at me, I could see her chin was trembling. Isaac stuck his tongue out at me and started running. I chased after him as he ran through the living room, and then the kitchen, where I was stopped by Honey's 409-smelling hand.

"What is going on with you two? Stop chasing your brother." Honey went back to spraying the counter with the stinky cleaner and wiping it down with a sponge. I didn't understand what she was trying to clean up; there wasn't anything there besides the shiny Formica.

"Honey, Isaac was mean to Aunt Aggie. He called her names and kicked her really hard. He said she was dumb," I stomped my foot to keep from crying. "But Aunt Aggie's not dumb, right? She's the best Monopoly player in the whole world." I stretched my arms out for emphasis.

Honey wiped her hands off on a towel, then brushed my hair away from my eyes. "Where is Agnes?"

"Maybe she's still at the table. Isaac messed up the game, too."

Honey gave me that look that meant she knew I was just tattling, before she went into the dining room. I clamped my teeth onto my lower lip, then followed her. Aunt Aggie was sitting slumped in her chair, sniffling and hiccupping. The game pieces were still sat scattered around her. She reminded me of the day Joey started crying really hard during indoor recess because the bigger boys in the class ran through the pile of Lego's he was playing with and knocked down the tower he built. It was as high as his waist before it fell over and broke into a million Lego pieces all over the tile floor. Some pieces even went under the bookshelf.

Most kids would have tried to fight the people who ruined such a time-consuming creation. But not Joey. He just sat there on the tile with his legs folded behind him, his chin stuck to the top of his chest and started to cry. And here was my Aunt Aggie crying because some bully ruined her game. That bully was Isaac. I was going to have to punch him really hard for this one.

"Agnes, are you all right?" Honey sat in the chair next to her and touched her arm.

"Isaac — he kicked me really hard in the leg, and he flipped the game like this," Aunt Aggie stuck her finger under the Monopoly board and flicked it upward. The few remaining pieces and cards scattered across the table and onto the floor. They made the same sound on the wooden table that the Lego's made as they had skipped across the tile, ricocheting against the bottom shelf of the bookcase and slipping underneath, out of reach of even the smallest hand.

"Is your leg okay?" Honey handed Aunt Aggie a Kleenex.

"It hurts really bad. I think it might have a bruise." She leaned down to rub her leg for emphasis, just like Joey rubbed his eyes when Mrs. Rappaport had finally come back into the classroom.

"Why don't you go into the bathroom and wash your face, then get a drink? I'll talk to Isaac and Beth."

I sat down next to Honey after Aunt Aggie left the room. Isaac peaked around the edge of the doorway. Honey snapped her fingers at him, and then pointed to the chair. He crept into the room, trying to stay as far away from Honey as possible while his hands protected his butt. He sunk into the chair and immediately started tracing the lines in the table with his finger.

"Isaac," Honey said in her soft voice. I didn't hear her usual rattle, but I knew that she still wasn't going to talk about anything fun.

Isaac looked up at Honey with his puffy eyes. I could tell he had been crying, which probably meant he that he felt bad, but I was still mad at him.

"Why did you kick your Aunt Aggie?"

Isaac shrugged. "She called me a cheater, and I'm not a cheater. Just like Daddy's not a cheater. I'm just a really good winner."

Honey propped her grandmother's chin on her calloused hand and sighed. "Isaac, I know that things have been hard at home, but that doesn't mean you can kick people. You know better than to kick people and call them names, don't you?"

"Yeah, but she called me a name first." Isaac sat back in his chair with a huff and crossed his arms over his skinny body.

Honey was quiet for a few minutes while she studied our faces. She didn't know that I was studying hers, too, and I was scared of the thoughts I saw dancing in her eyes. "Kids, I have to tell you something about your Aunt Aggie which may be difficult for you to understand. But I need you to try, okay?"

We nodded together solemnly. What could be wrong with Aunt Aggie?

"Your Aunt Aggie will always think and act like an eight-year-old no matter how old she gets." Honey looked at us to see if we understood her. We didn't.

"Think about your Mom and Dad as grown-ups. They bought a house and they drive a car and they had kids and work jobs. Your Aunt Aggie will never be able to do any of those things."

I looked at Honey and nodded, though I didn't want to believe her. Aunt Aggie was the best aunt any kid could ever had. Why did that have to make something wrong with her?

"Why won't she ever grow up?" Isaac asked with his chin on the table. He had stopped pouting.

"Well, it's because of a very complicated thing that happened when she was born. It's hard to explain to you two. All you have to know is your Aunt Aggie is handicapped."

"But Aunt Aggie doesn't need a wheelchair." I knew handicapped people were either in wheelchairs or they talked really funny or had big eyes and foreheads. Aunt Aggie wasn't like any handicapped person I had ever heard of before.

"She's mentally handicapped, which means she's a lot slower at doing things than other people. That's why she can't be the banker when you play Monopoly, but that doesn't mean she can't play it. Handicapped people just need a little extra love." Honey smiled her warm smile at us and winked at Isaac.

"Grandma? I'm sorry I kicked Aunt Aggie. I didn't know she was handy-cat." Isaac's eyes were as wide and as serious as when he talked about Mom and Dad's fights.

"Well, I think you should apologize to her." Honey reached across the table and rumpled his hair. He made a face at her, but he seemed to be feeling better. "Kids, just remember that Aunt Aggie is sensitive about her handicap. There's no need to talk to her about it. Your Aunt Aggie is the way she is just because that's how she was born. There's nothing that can be done to change it."

"Honey, are there a lot of handicapped people?" I thought about Joey who never knew the answer in class, his really bad handwriting, and all the times he had to take his work home at night because he couldn't finish it in class like everyone else.

She thought for a minute. "I think there's a lot of slow people. You may even have some in your school. They just need a little extra help sometimes." Honey winked and smiled at us one last time before she went back into the kitchen.

Isaac's nod was slow and serious. I started picking up the pieces to the Monopoly game, and I was surprised when he started to help me. Isaac hated cleaning and picking up his toys. Mom was always yelling at him about his messy room. I grinned at him as he put the game board in the box and I slid the lid on.

"Beth, can you catch handy-cat? Like if I hug Aunt Aggie too much, will I get handy-cat, too?

I shook my head. "I don't think so. Honey said Aunt Aggie was born with it, so I think all handicapped people are born with it. It's probably like being born with brown hair. I can't give you brown hair by sharing my brush with you."

Isaac moved forward awkwardly as if he were about to hug me, but stopped when he remembered who I was.

"We should play Chutes and Ladders," he said after a moment of him staring at his big toe peeking out of a small hole in his sock. "Aunt Aggie likes that game. It's easy."

****

Back at school on Monday, I was still thinking about Isaac kicking Aunt Aggie, and I finally began to understand what the other kids meant when they called someone retarded. I didn't like the word at all. It was a mean word. It was a word I wished I had never learned.

I stared at the alphabet stretched across the top of the blackboard. I wondered if Mrs. Rappaport was going to spend the whole day on grammar and reading. We never did math until after lunch and recess, which made the mornings seem really long.

I looked away from the board and traced the back of my classmates' heads with my eyes. When I got to Joey, I couldn't help but to stare a little longer. There was something about him that didn't seem exactly right, as if his head were misshapen or the wrong size.

"Can anyone give me an example of a noun?" Mrs. Rappaport sashayed from the back of the room to the front, and watched every hand in the room go in the air, except for Joey's. He just stared at his book, his head getting a little lower, and his shoulders getting a little higher.

"Joey, can you tell us a word that is a noun?" Mrs. Rappaport was standing in front of him now, but he wasn't looking at her. He never looked adults in the face like other kids did. The ground was his favorite place to look.

Dog, I thought. House.

"Can you think of a noun, Joey?"

Book. Chair.

His head jerked to the side for a second, and then it sunk a little lower. He still didn't look at her.

"How about a contraction? Can you think of one of those?"

Don't, I thought, remembering all the times Honey had

yelled at Aunt Aggie just because she hadn't known any better. He can't.

"Well, if you can't think of anything, then you'll have to stay in during recess to practice your nouns and contractions." Mrs. Rappaport looked up at the rest of the class to call on someone else. I could hear some of the boys snickering as I watched Joey's shoulders shrink down even more just like Aunt Aggie's did when Honey yelled at her. Aunt Aggie and Joey Dunbar. They could have been two wire hangers hung next to each other in a closet full of big, thick coats on sturdy, wooden hangers.

When the bell rang for recess, Joey sat in his seat and put his head on his folded arms. I could tell he was trying not to cry. I thought that maybe since at least once a week he had to stay in to learn something that he'd be used to it, but he wasn't.

I took a long time finding my coat, and even longer to button it. By the time I was done, all the other kids in my class were running down the hall toward the recess doors, while the playground moms blew their whistles at the stomping feet.

I thought of Aunt Aggie when she called me her favorite niece, when she hugged me too tight or kissed my cheek a million times in a row. I thought of Monopoly and Chutes and Ladders, and how all the boys who were mean to Joey knew better, but Isaac really didn't. I thought of Mom and Dad fighting late at night, throwing things and breaking things, even gifts we made them or bought them from field trips.

I knew Aunt Aggie would never yell at me or throw something or break anything. She would never kick Isaac back or get mad that I always beat her at Monopoly.

She may cry, but she would never get mad.

Joey, he never got mad either, even when the boys knocked

down his Lego tower, or tripped him on the playground. I looked at Joey with his head bent over some dittos, scratching his pencil tip against the page, tearing holes in the paper when he tried to erase. I reached my hand to my neck and began to pull the zipper back down, and take off my coat. Through the closed windows, I could hear the other classmates laughing on the playground. They played tag and kickball and all kinds of games in the chilly air, wearing the tennis shoes they tied themselves, and the mitten they never lost, and for once I felt that it was okay that I wasn't among them.

5.
Bye Bye Blackbird
Allen Kopp

The year Nellis Folts was eleven years old was the year he decided he would enter the school talent contest. He chose Bye Bye Blackbird for the number he would perform, and he wouldn't just stand there and move his lips to some stupid record the way some people did. He would actually sing the song. He asked Miss Mullendorfer, the assistant music teacher, to accompany him on the piano and she readily agreed, saying that she thought it was "simply splendid" that a boy like Nellis, who was usually so standoffish, was going to participate in something she knew was going to be "lots of fun."

"I'm not doing it for fun," he said. "I'm doing it for the prize money."

That evening when Nellis told his mother at the dinner table that he was going to perform in the talent show, she was less than enthusiastic.

"Are you sure you want to be up there on the stage in front of all those people?" she asked. "They'll laugh at you."

"I know. They laugh at me anyway."

"I didn't know you could sing."

"Well, I can."

"I've never heard you."

"I want you and father to come to the talent show. You can hear me sing then."

"I'm sure your father will be too tired to go out after having worked all day, but I'll try to come if it's a night I'm free."

"You're free every night."

For two weeks before the talent show, he practiced Bye Bye Blackbird every night in front of a full-length mirror in his bedroom, with hand gestures and a couple of dance steps that he made up himself. He sang in a quavery tenor that sometimes verged on the soprano:

Pack up all your cares and woes. Here I go, singin' low. Bye bye blackbird!
Where somebody waits for me. Sugar's sweet and so is she. Bye bye blackbird!
No one here can love or understand me. Oh, what hard-luck stories they all hand me!
So make the bed, light the light! I'll be home late tonight. Blackbird byyyye byyyye!

At the end of the song, he held out his arms and went down on one knee.

For his clothes, he would wear black pants, a white shirt, and, from a trunk in the attic, a decades-old yellow sport jacket with wide shoulder pads and a red-and-yellow bow tie. Just the thing.

The night of the talent show brought with it heavy rains and thunderstorms. Nellis's mother heard on the radio that storm warnings had been issued, but Nellis was not to be deterred. At six o'clock, one hour before the talent show was to begin, he put on his yellow plastic patrol-boy raincoat and, with his satchel containing the clothes he was going to perform in, walked the half-mile to school. He was soaked all the way through when he got there but was gratified to see that a lot of people had already shown up and taken their seats in the auditorium. The school was abuzz with excitement, in spite of the weather.

Without speaking to anyone, Nellis went into the deserted boys' room to prepare. He took off his raincoat and set his satchel on the floor and opened it. His hair was still wet, so he took a wad of paper towels and dried it off the best he could and poured some Vitalis into his palm, rubbed his hands together and smoothed down his thick mess of dark hair. He then combed his hair exactly the way Sammy Davis Jr. would have combed his if he had been there. He felt certain that anybody who owned a television set could not fail to make the comparison.

After dressing, he checked himself in the mirror and, when he was satisfied with the way he looked, especially the bow tie, he went "back stage," where he and all the other contestants had been told to gather at seven o'clock sharp to draw their numbers out of a hat to determine in what order they would appear on stage. When he picked his number from the hat and realized he was last, his heart did a little thump-jump inside his ribcage. But no matter, he told himself. He didn't mind being last; he would be freshest in the minds of the judges.

To begin the show, Mrs. Pepper, the music teacher, went out on the stage and waved her flabby arms to shush the audience. She was only four-and-a-half feet tall and almost as wide. Somebody in back of the auditorium whistled at her and yelled "Oh, baby!" but she pretended not to hear.

"Welcome to the annual school talent show!" Mrs. Pepper said in her whiny voice, training her myopic gaze on the middle distance. "It looks like we've got a capacity crowd! I'm happy to see that so many of you have braved the bad weather to be with us tonight! And I don't think you'll be disappointed! We've got a great show for you!"

The public address system squawked and sputtered, eliciting whistles and hoots from the audience.

She tapped on the microphone before continuing. "To make our competition a little more interesting," she intoned, "our first-place winner, as decided by our three judges, will win a prize of fifty greenbacks. Our second-place winner will win twenty-five greenbacks, while our third-place winner will receive a complementary pass for dinner for two at the Lonesome Pine Restaurant and Grill on Highway 32."

"Woo-woo-woo!" somebody in the audience yelled. Mrs. Pepper frowned for a moment before resuming her smile. "So, without further adieu," she said, "we now bring to you our little show."

The first contestant was Cecelia Upjohn, wearing lots of makeup, even though she was only twelve years old, and a skin-tight, glittery costume with red-white-and-blue diagonal stripes. She twirled her baton to a recording of I'm a Yankee Doodle Dandy, all the time with a fixed, doll-like grin on her face. When she tossed the baton high above her head, she somehow caught it without even looking at it. She finished her routine with a perfect split, one leg in front and the other behind as she went down on the floor with seemingly no effort at all. The audience rewarded her with resounding applause.

Then Ralph Krupperman with his hair the color of a new penny and Belinda Cornish took to the stage to do their Fred Astaire and Ginger Rogers dance routine. He wore a tuxedo with a swallow-tail coat and she a curly blond wig and a satiny white dress that clung to her immature body and dragged the floor. He flung her around and around at a dizzying pace to keep time with the music as the tails of his coat flapped and she tried hard to keep from falling. After a frenetic five minutes, the music ended and the routine was over. Ralph and Belinda clasped hands and smiled like onscreen lovers as they took their bows and exited stage left to polite applause.

When Curtis Bellinger came onto the stage, a questioning murmur arose from the audience because he carried a chair in one hand and a saw in the other. What was he going to do? Saw the chair in half? He carried the chair to the middle of the stage and set it down. Then he sat on the chair, put the saw between his knees, and, producing a violin bow, began playing Some Enchanted Evening. The audience was transfixed as the mournful sounds of the saw carried over their heads and out the doors into the rainy night. When the song was over, the audience applauded enthusiastically—more for the novelty and daring of the act than for its musicality.

As Curtis Bellinger was leaving the stage, a huge crack of lightning caused everybody to gasp and the lights to flicker, but the lights stayed on, and the moment of danger, if that's what it was, was forgotten in the wake of the next act.

Three large-for-their-age girls, who looked enough alike to be sisters but weren't, came onto the stage, their hair in snoods and dressed in women's army uniforms. They stood side-by-side, looking silly and self-conscious as they waited for their music to begin and, when it did, they began swiveling their hips and moving their arms like marionettes. They moved their lips to Boogie-Woogie Bugle Boy, while everybody, even the most naïve person in the audience, knew they weren't really singing.

The next act was Gus Goldblatt, a fifth grader who already weighed over two hundred pounds and wore men's clothes. His grandfather had started teaching him the accordion when he was only two years old and since that time he had become steadily more proficient with that instrument. He favored the audience with Lady of Spain, segueing smartly into I'm Just a Vagabond Lover. The audience was most appreciative.

Gus Goldblatt's exit brought Bertha Terhune to the stage. She was dressed in a black, full-body leotard with red ribbons in her hair and what appeared to be a bedroll under her arm. She curtsied in the direction of the audience, and, spreading out the bedroll that was really a tumbling mat, began her routine. She did a series of cartwheels, then forward somersaults and backward somersaults. She jumped into the air one way and then the other, twirled, twisted, leapt, spun, and turned, all with the agility of a flea and so fast that she was only a blur. The audience hooted and whistled.

Nellis watched all the acts from the wings as he waited to go on. He stood near a window and was aware of the storm, but what the weather might or might not do was the least of his worries. He knew he could remember all the words to Bye Bye Blackbird, but what he was worried about was "putting the song over," as they say. The audience had sat through a lot of acts. Would they be ready for his? Would they laugh at him, as his mother had said? Would they boo him off the stage? Suddenly he wanted the whole thing to be over and to be back home where it was safe and quiet. He took deep breaths, felt light in the head, and hoped he wouldn't be sick.

Miss Mullendorfer was standing beside him with her sheet music when Mrs. Pepper came to him and told him it was time for him to go on. He took a deep breath and walked out onto the stage. When he was installed behind the microphone, he looked out at the audience and tried to smile and they looked back at him, waiting to see what he was going to do. Two hundred eyes trained just on him, waiting for him to begin. Could he remember how the song began?

When Miss Mullendorfer from the piano played the little intro she had worked out, Nellis opened his mouth to let out the first notes. That's when the storm hit with all its force and fury. The row of windows behind the audience blew inward as if from an explosion. The audience screamed, a prolonged wail of terror, and, as if being awakened from a dream, jumped to their feet and began running in every conceivable direction, except toward the exits and safety.

Nellis was stunned. He didn't know what was happening. He looked over at Miss Mullendorfer at the piano to see if she might give him some cue as to what he should do, but she was gone. He was all alone on the stage, grasping the microphone stand in both hands. The thing sputtered and sparked. He might have been electrocuted if the power hadn't failed at that moment, bringing him to the reality of the situation. He was just able to make his way out of the building in the dark as the roof was picked up and deposited someplace else and the walls around him began to collapse like a house of cards.

6.

Delivered
Robert McGuill

Grampa thinks the mailbox is magic. He doesn't know it's Toby who makes it so. Toby likes to slip treasures into the mailbox when Grampa isn't looking, then watch from his bedroom window as the old man shuffles out onto the porch and claps his hands, smiling at what he finds.

Sometimes it's evening when Toby does this. Sometimes it's morning, when Grampa is still in his striped pajamas, grumping around in his terrycloth robe and old brown slippers.

"My heavens!" the old man will shout, bending down for a look, his white hair falling in strands over his forehead. "Look what the mailbox brought us this time!"

Sometimes the old man finds a greeting card. Other times he finds a big red apple that Toby's plucked from Jesper's orchard across the road. Once he found a mewing kitten, a tiny calico he named Buddy, who now shares his big wooden bed with him at night.

Toby likes to surprise Grampa. He likes to see Grampa smile. Sometimes when Grampa is cooking dinner, or in his study reading, or taking a nap with Buddy because he's worn out from the day's doings, Toby sneaks off to town on his bicycle to fetch something special for him.

Once, Toby came back with a chocolate shake. He got the shake from the soda fountain in Skiffington's Apothecary, and Melanie, the counter girl with the pretty red hair, packed it in a little bucket of ice for him. She even put her finger to her lips, and winked at him and said, "Don't worry, Toby. I won't tell your grampa. It'll be our secret."

Toby pedaled that chocolate shake back down the dirt road to Grampa's house as fast as his legs would go! As hard as his muscles would pump! His shirt was sweaty by the time he got home, but the ice in the bucket was still icy. When Grampa woke from his nap, the milkshake was waiting for him in the magic mailbox.

"Look here, Toby boy!" Grampa whooped, clapping his hands. "Look what the mailbox brought us!"

But it's the truth. Grampa's mailbox is different from everybody else's. It has wooden feet and ears. A gabled lid with a curved bill. A glass pane fitted into its back panel so you can see the surprises that lay inside.

Grampa's magic mailbox sits on the porch next to the front door like a little wooden soldier. Like it's there to guard Toby and Grampa from anything bad that could ever happen. Even the house number that's painted on its sturdy white chest reminds you of the way real soldiers wear their names on their uniforms.

On Saturday mornings, after breakfast, Grampa likes to sit outside with a cup of coffee. Buddy lies balled-up in his lap, and the two of them look out over the fields, listening to the birds sing, or close their eyes against the rising sun and doze to the warming hum of tractors in faraway fields.

Sometimes Grampa leafs through his newspaper while Buddy naps. Sometimes Toby sits beside Buddy and Grampa in the cane rocking chair that used to be Gramma's, and reads the comic books he's bought in town at the drugstore with his allowance.

Toby knows some grownups who think comic books are bad for you. But Grampa's not like that. Grampa doesn't mind what you read, as long as it's not disrespectful or blasphemous.

"My," he'll say in his crackly, old man's voice, looking over Toby's shoulder. "That looks pretty good, Toby. Mind if I borrow it for a while when you're finished?"

Toby and Grampa like to wait for the mailman. The mailman's name is Foster Newman. Foster wears a white pith helmet and sunglasses, and carries a leather satchel whose thick brown strap cuts deep into the shoulder of his blue uniform. In the summertime, Foster wears creased blue shorts with stripes down the side, and thin, black knee-high stockings that cling to his chicken legs.

Toby thinks if he were a postman, he would never wear shorts like Foster Newman's. Not even if somebody paid him. "How do!" Grampa says with a nod when he sees Foster come striding up the walk with the mail.

"Morning there, Mr. Everett!" Foster always comes back. "Good looking afternoon, wouldn't you say?"

Grampa always thanks Foster for delivering the mail and bids him cheerful weather and a fine day before he goes. When Foster's gone and the mail truck scoots off down the road in a puff of dust, Grampa will turn to Toby and say, "That Foster's a good egg. It can be a hard job, what he does."

Lately, Grampa seems quiet when the mail comes. Why this is, Toby doesn't know. The two of them are doing fine, Toby thinks, and have been for a long time now.

"We're doing fine, right Grampa?"

Grampa turns and gives him a kindly smile. "You bet we are, son," he says. "We've got each other, don't we?"

Toby remembers a long time ago, before the mailbox was magic, when letters came filled with anxious news about his mother and father. He remembers how quiet Grampa and Gramma got after reading the letters, and how for days afterward they shuffled around the house with troubled faces.

Toby doesn't really remember his mother and father anymore. But he does remember the quiet looks. The cautious whispers that went back and forth between his gramma and grampa. He remembers how Grampa took him for a walk one afternoon and held his hand and promised him that everything would be all right. That they would all look after one another. Toby believed Grampa because he knew Grampa would never lie. But just to be safe, when they got back from their walk Toby cast a spell over the mailbox and made it magic.

"What do you wish the magic mailbox would bring you now?" Toby says to Grampa as the old man ushers him up to his bedroom that night.

Grampa is mounting the stairs with wheezing breaths. Pulling at the wooden banister rail hand-over-hand, like a fisherman hauling in his net. "I wish it would bring me two good knees," he says.

He eases down on the old pine floor next to the bed and presses his hands together, his fingers pointing toward heaven. He still helps Toby with his prayers at night.

"No, really," Toby says. "What do you wish?"

Grampa looks at him, straight and uncomplicated. A look that goes right to the center of Toby's heart. "Okay," he says with a tender nod. "I wish it would bring the light of the world to all who need it."

Toby frowns. This isn't the sort of answer he's looking for. It goes outside the rules. Grampa knows as well as anybody that the magic mailbox can only bring things like apples and milkshakes and kittens.

"But really, Grampa!"

Grampa smiles and pats Toby on the head. "That's enough for tonight," he says. "We're tired. It's late, and growing boys need their rest."

Grampa urges Toby to fold his hands, and Toby does. Together they lower their heads and pray the Lord their souls to keep.

"God bless and forgive those we love," Grampa says. "And may their souls find everlasting peace."

"Amen," Toby says.

Grampa rises and gives Toby a kiss on the forehead, and after he's tucked the covers snugly beneath Toby's chin, he tells the boy goodnight.

"Good night, Grampa."

Toby rolls onto his back when Grampa's gone and opens his eyes, staring into the darkness, fretting over the old man's wish. It was easy stealing apples from Jesper's orchard, and making milkshakes and kittens appear. But the light of the world?

He wants Grampa to wish for something else. Something not so hard. He thinks that if you wish for a thing so big and shapeless you can't get your arms around it, it will only make God mad.

Toby remembers wishing for his parents' return, and waiting for the magic mailbox to bring a letter that said they were still alive.

A week later, a phone call came with the news that they had been found dead.

Toby doesn't want Grampa to disappear the way his mother and father did. Or die in a hospital ward with tubes in his nose like Gramma. So he slips out of bed, and tiptoes down the hall to implore the old man to change his mind.

The dim lamp on Grampa's nightstand is still burning, and when Toby peeks through the crack in the door he can see Grampa kneeling at the bedside, elbows propped on the bedcovers not far from Buddy, who's curled in a furry little ball, sleeping.

The old man's fingers are knotted in prayer. His eyes are closed, and his lips are trembling as if he's just stepped out of a meat locker.

Toby panics when he realizes Grampa is probably asking the Lord the same thing he asked of the magic mailbox, jinxing himself twice over. But before he can warn the old man, Grampa lifts his hand in the sign of the cross.

Toby lies awake all night worrying about Grampa, and the next day he stays close to home, guarding the magic mailbox so Foster Newman can't deliver the bad news that's sure to come. His vigilance pays. Foster Newman brings only a magazine that day, the National Geographic. But when the chicken-legged postman scoots away in his dusty white truck, Toby thinks, what about tomorrow? What about the weeks and months ahead when school starts and Grampa's home alone, left to fend for himself? Who'll protect him then?

He wraps his arms around his knees and shivers. He has a bad feeling about what's to come. He's afraid something dark and fearful is on the way.

There was talk once, after Toby's Gramma died, of Toby living with another family. Distant relatives of Toby's dead mother. But Grampa would have none of it. He assured the distant relatives that he would be cold in his grave before he allowed that to happen.

"I'd have to be dead and buried", he'd said solemnly, "before I ever turned out my own flesh and blood."

Toby just hopes Grampa hasn't done them in with his ungrantable wish. He worries that if the Lord is mad enough at Grampa for asking the impossible, Grampa will die and the distant relatives will come looking for him.

Toby knows Grampa would cling to life, cling to the very grass over his grave and refuse to be shoveled under, if he thought that his dying would leave Toby at the mercy of strangers. But Toby also knows you can't win a tug-of-war with an angry God.

That evening, while the old man nods in front of the television set and night falls across the fields, Toby slips out onto the porch in his bare feet and pajamas. Quietly, he descends the stairs, creeps around the house, and steals his way into Grampa's tool shed. When he emerges moments later, he has four empty fruit jars clutched to his chest.

The jars clack and rattle in Toby's arms as he hurries down the dirt road to Jesper's orchard. But he's smiling now. Grinning like the Cheshire cat. He leaps down into the dewy culvert, dashes up the other side, and vaults the broken rails of Jesper's whitewashed fence.

If Grampa could see Toby now he would think he was looking at a shadow. A night spirit moving among the trees, scratching at the sky as if trying to steal a fistful of stars. But Grampa doesn't see Toby. Grampa is asleep in his chair in front of the television, and has no earthly notion of the surprise that awaits him.

An hour has passed.

"Toby?" The old man shuffles onto the porch, worn and tired-looking, and the screen door clatters shut behind him, the floorboards creaking under his feet.

"Toby!"

"I'm right here, Grampa."

Grampa turns, startled, nearly stumbling over Toby.

There's a slowness to his old man's body tonight, as if it's burdened with the weight of too many cares, but when he looks down and sees Toby curled up in the chair that used to be Gramma's, he smiles. Relieved.

"Why are you sitting in the dark, son?"

Toby hesitates, then speaks up happily. "I'm not."

"You're not?"

"No."

Grampa scratches his head. "Well," he says, stuffing his fists into the pockets of his robe, "you could've fooled me."

Toby looks up at the wrinkled old man and laughs. He tugs away the burlap sack he's used to hide the magic mailbox, and reveals, with a theatrical flourish, the treasure concealed inside.

"Look, Grampa!" he says. "Look what the magic mailbox brought you!"

The old man squints, perplexed. He clutches the belt on his terrycloth robe, stoops, and brings his stubbled face close to the glass. As he looks in, pinpoints of light dance in the lenses of his steel-rimmed spectacles, and his thin, bloodless lips fumble open in a childlike smile.

"It's what you wished for, isn't it?"

Grampa doesn't answer. He just stands there, trembling. Eyes thawing in the iridescent glow of the swirling fireflies, the light of the world before him, shining out to all who need it.

7.
Family Sightings
Melodie Corrigall

Sightings set our family apart: they are our speciality. Not just any sightings, sightings of the "top of the heap" as Mom puts it—Elvis, movie stars and the Devil himself.

We even catch sight of celebrities whose names we don't know. "Isn't that the woman that played the wife of the guy who fell over the cliff in Disaster," Mom cries, leaning out the window to catch a last glimpse as the gas station shrinks in the distance. Dad is in a mean mood and refuses to slow down.

"Check out the guy at the Deli counter—I think it's the fellow who got off on that grow-op charge," that from Pebbles, who is into newspaper people and politics and things like that.

"He's in the Bahamas by now," Dad grumbles.

Notice a pattern here? Dad is not with us. When I said our family is good at sightings, I should have said our little family—my Mom Mellie, Pebbles and me. Dad has never had a sighting... the best he can do is notice some guy who he thinks he used to work with at The Dairy Queen.   And even when we point out someone, Dad just adjusts his glasses, squints at them and comes up with something negative such as, "What would they be doing here?" or "Why would a person like that wear a ripped jacket" or worst of all, "For goodness sakes Mellie, the Devil doesn't exist."

Well, I used to think that too, but seeing is believing.

In the past, Dad was mostly neutral: he just shrugged and waited outside the store for us to do a double check. But he's neutral no more.

Now—now that it matters—now that we are going up against our larger family—the "Never buy anything that isn't for sale side," as Mom describes them. The side that won't even invite us over to a party when Uncle Jim's boss is going to be there: "Afraid we won't know what fork to use," says Mom.

Suddenly, as Pebbles puts it, "We are in the family's viewfinder," and they are trying to clamp our mouths shut. They want us to turn our backs on what could be the chance of our lives. Dad's to blame because he mentioned it to Uncle Jim when Jim came into the hardware store on a complaint mission. As Dad put it, Uncle Jim just up and snorted. "Say you're kidding," and then he went as white as a mushroom. "No way," he shouted. "No way. I'm running for council next year and Betty has to teach. We'd be the laughing stock."

No surprises. If it's good for us, you can be sure Uncle Jim will be against it. I don't know how he and Mom came from the same parents: she likes to laugh, shake things up, tease her customers and soak in the sun out back near the little pool she and Dad made. Uncle Jim and Aunt Betty never sit out back: "That's not a pool Mellie. It's a hole in the ground with plastic covering," Uncle Jim says.

Jim and Betty spend their weekends cleaning and fixing their property. "It's essential in my position at the bank to have a neat home and garden," he says. The house even has a name 'Summer's End' but they live there all year. Duh!

In fact, I was glad Uncle Jim was against us taking up the offer. It proved we were on the right track. When I listened to him and Mom argue (even if I'd been in my room I could have heard every word. In our house a shout from the kitchen echoes right up to the bathroom, (even with the shower on) and he said, "People will think that my sister is some celebrity freak." I just smiled. But then when he called up the stairs to me crouched on the landing, "You'll be the laughing stock of the school, you nit. Get your mother off this plan," I began to wonder.

"Any publicity is good publicity," scoffed Pebbles when I told her, but she's no longer in school. In junior high, it's best to play it cool; when you stick your head up you might get a pie in the face. That's just an example, like in an old Chaplin comedy. We don't have pies in the cafeteria unless you're thinking pizza. But it could be anything, a book or someone's day-old sandwich. You get the point.

Sightings are just one of the ways we don't stick to a pattern. Over the years, there have been a few comments about my Mom. Sometimes guys I bring home ask, "What are those Christmas decorations still doing in the living room?" or "Isn't it the wrong season for Halloween?"

But to explain our present chance for glory. After Uncle Jim left and I got into bed, I started thinking. Usually I'm out like a light but that night the idea just kept going around in my head. First off, the excitement and a rush, like jumping off the side of the house: we'd be in the newspaper, and the Saturday section at that. Maybe, we'd be on the radio or the local TV. Mom says this is the sort of story the "media picks up." It's a 'man bites dog' story she says, although we never sighted a famous dog.

Then, well, what would stop us, because Mom and Pebbles are hilarious when they get started? The Rentners from next door roar with laughter when Mom imitates Mayor Dickens. Mrs. Rentner says Mom and Pebbles could be on a TV show. So maybe one of the talk shows would get hold of us and invite us down. You're treated like stars. You stay in a fancy hotel with a pool and eat at some great BBQ rib place. Then some family would be looking at us and saying "Isn't that Danny and Pebbles and their Mom who do all the sightings?" and when I went back to school, heads would turn. Mr. Picket would announce it on the PA system in the Monday roundup. First of the news, "Welcome back, Danny, from your trip to..." like New York or somewhere. "We have a TV star in our midst," he would say and all day when I walked down the hall or stopped at my locker, kids would high-five me or give me the Brandy High snap. The younger kids would cluster in the corner, whispering, afraid to come up and talk to me. After all, I had been on TV; they hadn't even been on the radio.

"Whispering what?" Uncle Jim says when I explain it to him. "They'll be whispering that you're all crazy. Like those people who read the National Enquirer not waiting in line at the cashier but who buy it and read it at home. The people who go down to the place Elvis lived and see his ghost."

I began to get uneasy about what might happen at school. Welcel Spry, who always gets things going, would have everyone snickering and shoving me until finally Picket would come out of his office and shout, "Cut it out boys" and everyone would clam up but as I passed the word "buzz head" would sting like a horse fly and every time I turned, silence.

Who to believe? Mom or Uncle Jim? "It's a dilemma," Pebbles says. That is something that sounds good but then seems bad when you get closer and it has horns. You get on it sort of like riding a bull at the rodeo or a bucking bronco. Well a bronco doesn't have horns but it's pretty wild. When you get on you could win the prize money, or it could turn out bad. Well, a lot worse than bad, you would be totally squashed. Just like on the kid's cartoons but you wouldn't bounce back. So there we are, on the fence.

Mom is set on us going, so it's not just up to me, and Pebbles says,

"What the heck, we can't be worse off and who wants to stay in this loser of a town anyhow." She plans to head to Vancouver in the spring and even if you were in the paper or on a show, there are so many people in that city that you could hide out for ten years if you wanted. Not like Becker—it's so small that when you walk down the street everyone knows you. If you feel friendly and give a wave to everybody, you could have your arm in a cast by the end of the day you'd be so sore.

So if we agree to have the interviews, the story will appear the next week in the local paper. And then it is sure to be picked up nationally, Cindy, our local reporter says.

What's all the fuss about? You ask. Why do they want our stories? Because of our sightings, of course. I'll give you two examples.

First, Elvis. We were going down to the states—to Bellingham—to shop. We were waiting at the border. It takes so long now because in New York, three planes went into the Tower and it was guerrillas so they are watching at the border. (We might sight them but I'm not sure what they look like.) Pebbles was reading her star magazine but she said the sun was hurting her eyes so she started to check out cars and suddenly she said, "My God, there's Elvis;" so Mom and I turned around quick and we tried to see. But just at that Moment Dad jerked the car ahead, and Mom said, "Wait, for goodness sakes, wait." But Dad hates waiting in line and was in a huff. "He's in the other line, two over," shouts Pebbles, leaning out and pointing to a real clunker. "Well, of course he would be in a car like that. He doesn't want anyone to recognize him."

Would he be older? Not with modern medicine. He's rich and could have had a whole bunch of operations. Still, he looked pudgy like Uncle Jim, and leaning in to the driver (of course he wouldn't be driving himself) so the custom inspector couldn't see him as well as we could. He ended up getting right through so we lost him as quick as we found him.

Even more impressive was when we saw the Devil. He had a small red car and was driving by himself (who would go with him?). He was as short as I am, with a little black pointy beard and had stopped at the red light. "If he were the devil, wouldn't he go through," Dad argued, but duh! Of course not. He doesn't want to be noticed.

We talked for months about what he was doing there and why he had a red car. "He was sort of spitting at the wind," Mom said, but I never understood what that meant.

The Devil and Elvis are just two examples. We've had lots more sightings: an old lady Mom recognized from Coronation Street, the guy who played Batman, and a Siamese cat from a TV commercial. It goes on and on which is why our local paper wants our story. But time is running out. If we don't decide by Saturday to do the interview Cindy says she's done with us.

I don't know how it will turn out but whatever happens, things will never be the same. You can't have chances like this come at you and not feel the speed bump. Mom says, "either you take it and you end in the fast lane or you let it pass by and your name fades from history. In that case, you can be sure no one will ever be sighting you. "

8.
Fish Tale
Terry Sanville

Señora Sanchez was all right, even though she sometimes smelled funny and had wrinkles on her brown face that were deeper than the cracks in the concrete patio my dad tried installing that summer. She had her own special way of sitting in a faded canvas chair, round-shouldered body hunched over the fish bucket strategically placed between varicose-veined legs, legs fortunately covered most of the time by a flowery sundress. Beneath the deep brim of her straw hat were a set of opaque black eyes that glowed with a strange knowing, and she was quick to laugh and joke around, even with us kids; except when she was listening to a ball game and her beloved Dodgers were losing, which during the 1958 season they were doing a lot.

"That stupido Koufax will never make it in the majors," she complained. "He'll be back playing Triple A before the All Star game."

You could find Señora Sanchez just about every day, except Sundays, holding court from her spot at the very end of the Huntington Beach pier, yakking away with Mr. Triviani the retired barber, Jack Swank, an out-of-work mechanic living off his wife's barmaid income, or with Joe Blanco of unknown occupation who couldn't speak any English. She'd be there before the early surfers slid their boards into the cold gray morning surf and she'd still be there after the lifeguards locked up their lonely towers for the night. From her spot, backed into the corner railing, she could see everybody coming and going and shoot the breeze with old geezers, kids and families alike. They'd ask her how the fish were biting, about her grandkids, especially the sickly Juanita that she helped take care of nights when her daughter had to work as a Police Dispatcher; and the old ones would say how they still missed her husband Ernesto who had passed away right after the Korean War.

Now, for Señora Sanchez, fishing was only an adjunct to her social life on the pier. When she actually caught something she'd likely give it away to anyone who expressed interest, mostly Mexican families with lots of kids. Some days I would find her bucket full of perch, some days a few mackerel; cat food, my Grandmom called them; or an occasional dogfish or sand shark. It was a wonder that she caught anything with the rig she used: an old deep-sea rod with the sections held together with black electrical tape and a rusting reel with a huge star drag. In the early mornings, sometimes with my help, she'd scavenge the pier and beach for bait, finding mostly pieces of squid or the guts from a cleaned fish, but also discarded sandwiches from the garbage cans that I rifled through the day before, looking for empty pop bottles.

One afternoon we were talking about baseball and her family back in Tampico, Mexico. Her fishing rod was at its normal place, leaning against the railing with the end braced against the back of her chair. I noticed that the line had gone slack, so I reeled it in for her and discovered that the bait was gone along with the hook and lead weight. From her ancient tackle box Señora Sanchez extracted a new sinker and a triple barbed hook and attached them to the line, holding the hook close to her eyes to tie the knots with stubby fingers. The head of a mackerel with staring eyes was used for bait. She set the transistor radio down next to her chair and groaned softly as she pushed herself up and turned toward the end railing. Grabbing the rod with two hands, Señora Sanchez threw it back over her shoulder and heaved it toward the horizon. The line sailed outward and dropped into the gleaming Pacific about a hundred feet from the pier's end. She leaned her rod against the railing and was just about to slump back into her chair when there was a high-pitched whirring sound from the reel and the rod vaulted up off the pier decking. The only thing that kept it from going over the side was the last line guide next to where the reel was attached – it had snagged the top railing.

I grabbed the rod, pulled it in and handed it over to Señora Sanchez. The drag was off and the line was screaming, pointing straight at the horizon, and going out fast.

"Let her run, let her run, Lucinda!" an excited Mr. Triviani yelled. With the first whine from the reel, the normally lethargic pier contingent had crowded around us, yelling advice, the voice of a hundred experts.

"Could be a shark. It'll break your rod when it hits!"

"Ease on the drag or you're gonna lose 'im!"

"Cut 'im loose, whatever it is. It's too big for your tackle!" Señora Sanchez was braced against the railing, holding the end of the rod with both trembling hands and staring at the ocean. More than two hundred yards of her line was already gone when it went slack and she started to reel it in slowly, expecting to find nothing on its end. In a minute, the line snapped taunt, this time to the right, heading inland, and again she almost lost her rod over the railing. Whatever it was had doubled back and was heading for the shore in a zigzag path, jerking the rod every few minutes when it changed course.

Señora Sanchez was holding on for all she was worth, grinning but unable to move her hands from their position on the cork-covered handle for fear of losing their precarious grip. "Give 'im some drag," she hissed at me between clenched teeth, and I reached forward and spun the star wheel back half a turn. I was surprised that the thing even worked.

"Give 'im some more," she said, so I spun the drag another half turn and the speed of the line unwinding from the spool slackened. Her rod was almost pointed at the shore, somehow miraculously avoiding snagging anybody in the water, when it went slack again. This time, Señora Sanchez reeled it in fast before the fish had a chance to strike, and I gave the star drag another turn. When the fish hit with a vengeance, it came up at the surf line, exploding through the top of a six-foot wave right next to a surfer. The kid fell off his board in astonishment. The fish was maybe four feet long, a slender dagger of polished silver with distinctive chevrons along its body and a pointed snout. It momentarily writhed in mid-air, almost dancing on its tail across the curl of the wave before diving again. Señora Sanchez was now rapidly cranking the spindle, working the fish hard and not letting it run.

All during these events, the pier contingent was yammering advice, advancing opinions about what kind of fish it was, recalling their own fish stories that got more extraordinary with each passing moment, or talking about how they would prepare the beast for supper – covered in salsa, baked in a white wine sauce, stuffed with rice and shallots, or simply grilled on the backyard bar-be-que and served with lemon wedges.

Señora Sanchez had worked in the fish close to the pier and it was still fighting hard; the end of her rod was bent in an almost perfect "U" from the strain. As she struggled to pull it from the water directly below us, the end section of her rod broke away from the rest with a loud snap and again the fish almost yanked the rod out of her hands, hands that had cracked under the tension and were slowly seeping crimson onto the dirty cork handle.

Even with the shortened rod, Señora Sanchez kept reeling it in and at last it was close enough that I could grab the line and help haul the fish over the rail. It lay thrashing on the pier's rough planks, its tail slapping back and forth, long mouth with needle-sharp teeth and protruding lower jaw opening then snapping shut. Slowly its struggles slackened and finally its wild maniacal eyes were still.

The Grey Wolfe Storybook

"That's gotta be a barracuda by the looks of its mouth," said Mr. Triviani and Señora Sanchez just smiled. She was still holding the rod with both hands and finally unclenched her fists just and let it fall with a clatter.

"Ernesto used to call them sea wolves. They bring good luck when you eat them. I'm gonna have Joe Blanco smoke this one to kill the poisons then give some to Juanita. She can use the luck." The pier contingent murmured their assent and reluctantly went back to their camp chairs and transistor radios.

"You helped me, Sandy. You want some of this?" Señora Sanchez asked as she pried the triple hook out of the 'cuda's upper jaw with a pair of needle-nosed pliers.

"Naw, Grandmom doesn't like to cook fish, even though we're Catholic," I grinned and Lucinda grinned back, looking younger and stronger than I had seen her all that summer. By the end of August, she would bring Juanita along with her and they'd sit side-by-side, staring patiently at the ocean, waiting for their next piece of good luck to hook.

9.
Grandpa Fella Storyteller
Jon Moray

I was eight years old when my grandfather died of a sudden heart attack in his wooden rocking chair that was situated beside the fireplace in his living room.

My earliest memory of my grandfather, Grandpa Fella Storyteller, was at five when my parents dropped me off at his country home for the day, while they attended a wedding. I called him Grandpa Fella because he would always call my dad and any other man 'Fella.' He affectionately referred to me as 'Little Fella.' That day I was introduced to his wonderful stories of fantasy and science fiction; time travel was his passion. It was then when I added the 'Storyteller' part to his nickname.

He noisily settled in his chair and motioned me over with a pointed crooked forefinger protruding from his bony hand. A skeleton of a frame, with white, stringy hair, bi-focal glasses, flannel shirt, and jeans with patches on both knees was probably the best way to describe his appearance.

I hopped beside him in his seat that easily accommodated the both of us with room to spare. He thumbed through a loose leaf binder where his hand-written stories were housed and asked me if I wanted to hear a fantastic tale. I nodded with excitement as if I was a bobblehead doll. That day, he told a story about a boy that traveled back in time by spinning a coin counterclockwise to the year that was on the coin. I closed my eyes and the words that floated from his raspy voice guided me along on this fantastic journey. All the while, Grandpa Fella rocked the chair gently as if mimicking a spaceship battling subtle turbulence.

"Someday, I'm going to publish my stories and give books to all of my grandchildren," he said, with eyes that sparkled as if he saw his book-writing dream in my eyes.

"Why don't you use the computer to write, Grandpa Fella Storyteller?"

"I've never learned how to use those things. Besides, I enjoy the scratchy sound the pencil makes when it touches the paper." From that day on, every visit with Grandpa Fella included a time traveling story in his rocking chair that seamlessly segued into a spaceship when he was deep in his moving narrative. I struggled with the news of his departure. We had made quite a bond.

My parents and I arrived at his home that featured a deep wrap-around porch that sheltered the home from the boiling heat in the heart of summer. I exited the family sedan, leading the way through the front door and my scampering progress into his living room came to an abrupt halt when I saw Grandpa Fella's rocking chair.

As my parents sifted through important papers and remnants in his bedroom, I hurried to the chair as my way of paying homage to my grandpa. My momentum and clumsiness rocked the chair backward and almost upended. I exhaled deeply, allowing my loving memories of Grandpa Fella to swirl in my head. I closed my eyes and imagined him opening his binder, clearing the lingering saliva from his throat and uttering the first word of a highly anticipated tale. Suddenly, I heard his voice, no longer raspy, but clear. I opened my eyes to find only me in the vicinity.

"Close your eyes and enjoy the adventure," said Grandpa Fella, in a soft, reassuring tone, as my startled, rapid heartbeat simmered. I did as instructed as he began to spin a story of a man that was unexpectedly thrust into the future by way of a revolving door serving as a portal. The chair began to rock gently as he described peaceful aliens inhabiting Planet Earth and sharing secrets to a blissful planet. His craft of literary imagery flowed as his creation of well-intended aliens with elongated multi-colored heads and distorted slender bodies made me wish I could travel to that faraway place. I could see his worldly vision as if his ghostly thoughts were remotely transmitted into my brain.

"The end," Grandpa Fella Storyteller announced theatrically, with the promise of more stories as long as I occupied his magical chair. Stories that deserved to be heard and published.

I opened my eyes as my mom approached.

"What's going to happen to Grandpa Fella's easy chair," I asked, expecting an unfavorable answer.

"Grandpa wrote a will about a year ago. In it he said his rocking chair was to go to you. Your father and I discussed the matter and we decided the chair is way too big to keep in your room, so it will be kept in the basement. It's an old and beat up piece of furniture. Are you sure you want it?"

My mother looked at my freckled face and saw Grandpa's youthful enthusiasm in my deep blue marble eyes and crescent moon shaped smile. It was the same demeanor that glossed Grandpa Fella Storyteller's face whenever he discovered a new fantastic story idea.

"I'll take that as a yes," she said, as she lovingly stroked my hair.

As I grew older and the challenges of adulthood and responsibility increased, Grandpa Fella Storyteller's chair collected dust in the basement. I moved out of my folk's home, married, bought a house, and was an expectant father.

My wife had begun her third trimester when she announced her desire for a rocking chair to soothe the baby inside of her and eventually, after the birth. She told me she saw one that caught her eye on one of the shopping channels. Thoughts of Grandpa Fella's chair rocketed back to me like one of his stories. I told her I would look into a chair, grabbed the keys to my SUV, and sped over to my parents' home.

After typical kiss-on-the-cheek pleasantries with my mom, I informed her I would take the rocking chair home with me. A melodically enhanced 'halleluiah' echoed from her vocal chords as I hurried down the creaky basement steps. The chair was draped in an old bed sheet. I stripped away the linen and was floored by the refurbished, solid oak finish that gleamed under the fluorescent lighting.

"Your father and I were going to surprise you with it at the baby shower. I remember that chair being like a best friend to you and thought restoring it would make a great gift. But since the new mommy has a furniture craving, I say you take it now."

I thanked her with a bone cracking, bear hug embrace that would make a chiropractor proud. I carried the chair to my vehicle and carefully placed it inside. I got home and instructed my wife to cover her eyes as I positioned the chair in our living room.

"Okay, you can look now," I said, with anticipation.

She joyfully gasped and covered her mouth in euphoric laughter as I guided her to the chair.

"The baby has been uneasy and kicking up a storm this whole week. I can really use the easy motion now."

She slowly sat down and wiggled herself into maternal comfort. She breathed deeply as her eyes slowly closed like a theater curtain. She smiled as she gently rubbed her belly and I can only wonder if Grandpa Fella Storyteller had begun to narrate a wondrous tale to my little one inside.

10.
I Forget Who Was On Whose Side
J. J. Steinfeld

A long-ago schoolyard game of war
a battlefield or battleground, rebuilt in recollection,
words even now carrying and constructing memory
I forget who was on whose side
what the objectives were
we being young and blood-thirsty
unaware of formal tactics and strategies
or a warlike nature in historical hearts and minds
belligerent and *combative*
words unknown to our childish artlessness
none of us had yet read *Lord of the Flies*
or *Nineteen Eighty-Four*
or *All Quiet on the Western Front*
looked through the lenses of disquieting authors
not a single poem by a forgiving or an unforgiving poet
or even dabbled in cynicism or worldly sorrow
we were kids playing the primordial, the language rudimentary,
too young to kill, too old to forgive

following the leader, falling into place,
I remember that
and I remember
one boy in particular
because someone thought
he was effeminate, aloof,
and another boy, as fierce as a movie warrior,
led a mid-morning raid
on the remarkable-bodied non-combatant
I yelled for them to stop
retreat, surrender,
unavailing adult words,

and I was relieved that looks
were not knives
or I would have bled to death

that night I heard my father say
Europe is far away
and Hitler is dead
but my father did not sound safe.

11.
Jack Martin
Celia P. Ransom

Jack Martin is my grandson. He is named after his two grandfathers, both men of fine character. He is eleven years old and can be a handful at times. I never reared boys so it is often difficult for me to adjust to some of the things that boys are involved in—their unacceptable language, intense interest in sports and the fact that they do not consider manners extremely important, especially at this age.

Regardless, I have to puff up and explain that Jack is an extremely bright boy. He is articulate. (He would know the meaning of that word.) His math skills are far above average for his age and he has always been a reader. When a tot, he would fall asleep with books cluttering his bed. I recall when he was three years old, he and I were sitting on the deck at our cottage. He was on my lap and I was reading to him from the book NEMO. When I finished, he said, "Read it again, Grandma." For some reason I wondered if he knew any of the words in the book. I pointed to the word "father" and asked what that word said. He responded correctly. I inquired about two or three random words. Again, he answered with exactness. By age five, he could read just about anything. He was a natural.

Being bright, Jack can also be stubborn. He may not want to do the things that you want him to do. It is sometimes a struggle. He needs to be challenged and believe me, he himself, is quite a challenge. You can imagine my surprise that on his Christmas list he had written that he wanted to spend a day with me. Now understand, I am not a young grandmother—not at all. Why he would want to spend time with me, an old lady, was beyond my comprehension. Two hours was the most time we had ever spent together, just the two of us, and then he was bored with me. When he and his sister Cassie were with me together, that time was spent reprimanding the two because they constantly aggravated each other. It was not terribly pleasant. It was with some trepidation that I agreed to a day together, grandma and grandson. In early April we did so. I am still smiling!

I picked Jack up mid-morning. He looked as though he had just stepped out of the shower. He was gleaming with hair spiked and a brand-new hoodie.

He had specific things that he wanted to do that day. Going to a restaurant was at the top of his list. This was something that I did with his sister when we two "girls" went shopping. Did he want breakfast or lunch? He wasn't sure, so I suggested Big Boy as that would cover the bases. At Big Boy he decided on lunch. When the waitress took our order, he meticulously described how he wanted his burger designed. And yes, he would have fries. Throughout the meal we had conversation about family and the upcoming trip to visit his other grandmother in Texas. Lunch ended, he took out his wallet and proffered a five dollar bill to pay for his lunch. "No, Jack," I said. "It is my treat, part of your Christmas wish." Then he wanted to provide the tip. I told him that I had already left a sufficient amount. He looked at the bill, mentally calculated what I had placed on the table and agreed. He said, "I just want to be sure there is enough because the waitress was very nice to me." He was right, for she had treated him very kindly.

The next item on his agenda was to buy video games. We stopped at Wal-Mart. He had his own money to spend. He did not find anything that interested him other than a gift card that allowed him to play an online game. Our next stop was Game Stop. Here he quickly selected two sports games. He had a discussion with the sales clerk regarding the merits of wireless versus wired controller for his X-Box. The discussion concluded, Jack made his decision and we left.

Purchases made, I told Jack that I would like to stop by my house before I took him home. At that point he said, "But, Grandma, aren't we going to cook? You always cook with Cassie."

I said, "Oh, Jack, I hadn't planned on that." I thought for a moment and said, "Well, I was going to make corn bread for Grandpa's dinner so you could do that for me and then take some home." So he did. He had no difficulty following the directions on the box. I told him that even though he was making it from a mix that I would give him my secret for making good corn bread. He was not to tell, but a little sugar in the batter makes it taste better. He popped it in the oven and we waited for it to brown.

While he was with me at the house, he was still talking about his family's visit on Easter and the egg hunt. On Easter, I hide money-filled plastic eggs throughout the house for my grandkids. He remarked on what a good job of hiding them I had done this year and went about recalling the various places he had found the eggs. He grinned proudly over the one that he found in the oatmeal box. For an "old" grandmother I guess I did provide him with some fun that day.

All the way home in the car we talked. I told him stories about his mother, my daughter, when she was a girl. We discussed the jujitsu class that he was taking as well. I loved talking with him. There were no lulls. His conversation was of interest to me.

Then he asked, "What are you going to do tomorrow, Grandma?" I told him that I would be going to my writing group. He wanted to know all about the people in my group. I explained the make-up and that some were younger than I and some older. He wanted to know their names. I told him that four had published books. His questions became more intense wanting to know the names of their books and what the books were about. I gave him the background of each author and information on their publications. He listened to all of this with great interest. He wondered where he could buy the books. I am still not sure about his thinking on the subject but I was amazed at the amount of conversation that we had on the topic.

I have to say that I dropped off Jack at home with a happy heart. I do not know his thoughts but I had a great day. I saw a different child, one teetering on the brink of maturity. I saw a boy interested in what I had to say—a boy who asked good questions and was willing to listen to answers and explanations. We shared a mutual respect. He left me with a hug. I left him with great expectations for what he will become.

12.
Jada's Story
Mark Hudson

I found a courageous kid on-line;
it was a hurting kid who doesn't whine.
She's eleven and has a life of pain;
she gets terrible headaches in her brain.
Her diseases started when she was four,
but she is a kid anyone would adore.
Pictured with a puppy in her arms;
she seems oblivious to any harms.
She has a liver disease called PSC,
and Chron's disease since infancy.
She goes to the hospital on many occasions,
and her life is not much of a celebration.
But her parents enjoy each moment with her;
because death is something bound to occur.
Her mom created a website for others;
for courageous kids, fathers and mothers.
Heaven is a place where children will win,
where pain and suffering cannot get in.
There is no better place to be;
if only the rest of the world could see.

13.

Little Cup
Janel Mills

Today was a nice day.

The girls spent most of the day playing together all over the house. Phaedra put on a little show they call "Circus" for Bella while she took her bath. They sifted through the enormous pile of little figures and dolls and found the Special Agent Oso toys, reenacting an episode together before bedtime, each girl cracking up at the other one's silly song or plot twist. When I asked Phaedra to clean up her room before bedtime, she decided she wanted to make Bella's bed for her. She spread the blanket, arranged the pillows just so, and placed a few of Bella's favorite stuffed animals on top of the pillows. She couldn't wait for Bella to see it. When bedtime came, they asked to sleep together in Phaedra's bed. Although I vetoed it (because I prefer that they fall asleep before 2am), I nearly changed my mind when they walked hand-in-hand to Bella's room for the big reveal.

Like I said, today was nice. Tonight, however, was not as nice.

Bella was tired, and she's going through a bad cycle, as autistic kids tend to do, where things that were previously not that big of a deal are suddenly an enormous, tear-filled battle. Just getting her up the stairs to the bathroom to brush her teeth was a ten-minute ordeal filled with pleading, cajoling, and slightly raised voices. So when Phaedra kept telling Bella that she had put Bella's pink frog on her bed, Bella insisted that it was not there. When Phaedra proudly showed Bella what she had done for her as a special surprise, Bella rushed over to the pink frog, yelled "NO!" and started tossing the painstakingly arranged pillows and stuffed animals off the bed. In Bella's mind, her bed looked different; it wasn't right. Not right is upsetting. Not right is frightening. Bedtime is a hard transition for her to make, so everything needs to be exactly the same every night to make things go as smoothly as possible. A detail I forgot until the second that pink frog flew past my head as I turned to see Phaedra's face fall from anticipated delight to hurt, confused anger.

****

As much as I worry about how autism is affecting Bella, I worry equally as much about how it is affecting Phaedra. Since Bella's diagnosis, we've helped her understand that Bella isn't just a jerk who screams and loses it over little things in order to ruin everyone's day. Phaedra knows now that Bella's brain works differently than hers or mine. One day, as we were driving to my mom's house, Bella started having a full-blast, take-it-to-eleven, screeching meltdown because she dropped a toy somewhere in the car and neither she nor I could reach it. Phaedra hates the car meltdowns most of all because she can't go anywhere to escape them. Listening to Bella melt down hurts her physically (the screams are LOUD) and emotionally (she's a sensitive soul). When we finally pulled into my mom's driveway and I got Bella her toy, Phaedra asked me with a shaky voice why Bella reacted the way she did. I must have heard this or read this somewhere, because there's no way I was this clever on the spot, but this is what I told her:

"Everyone has a cup in their head. We pour all of our feelings, like happy, sad, mad, scared, anything, into that cup. Most people have regular-size cups. When you pour out your feelings into your cup, you have more than enough room for them. Bella has a cup, too, but her cup is little. When she pours her feelings out, her little cup can't hold all of them, and it overflows. Does that make sense, honey?"

Apparently it did, because she uses this story to explain to others how Bella is different. She shares it with teachers, friends, basically anyone who will stand still and listen to her talk about her family.

"My sister Bella has a little cup."

Since Bella started preschool, her social skills and communication have steadily improved. Part of that improvement is due to the new educational program and therapies she receives at school, as well as the incredible teachers and therapists carrying out those services. There is someone else, though, that deserves credit for the huge leap forward Bella has made verbally and socially this fall: Phaedra. While Bella gets speech and occupational therapy at school, she gets play therapy at home with her bossy older sister. Phaedra instructs Bella on how to play games and act out scenarios. She tells her what to say, what to do, and how to do things that other kids naturally know how to do. When I describe how Phaedra plays with Bella to her therapists and doctors, they are tickled and amazed.

But no one is more amazed or tickled than I. In the past four years, I've watched these girls go from two girls who were basically indifferent to each other to sisters who run around the house screaming and laughing hysterically over the silly games they've made up together.

"Okay, Bella, now you be Snoopy, and I'll be Lucy this time."

"Bella, do you want to play beauty shop?"

Shortly after Bella's diagnosis, I was chatting with a friend about their own experience with an autistic sibling. I told her about my worries that autism would ruin my girls' chances of being close, of having a great relationship. I told her I feared that Phaedra would resent Bella or be jealous of the attention she received, that they wouldn't get along and would be embarrassed of each other as they grew older. "But Janel, that stuff happens with ALL sisters. Do you really think if Bella was an average girl, they wouldn't have those problems?"

She's right. Sisters fight. They argue, they grow jealous of one another, they slam doors, they poke, they bite, and at times they firmly believe their life would be better off without their sister. They also hug, hold hands, giggle, perform crazy news shows, and help each other. They want to do things together, and worry when one is away. They're not best friends every single day, but they're also not just two people who happen to live in the same house and share the same parents anymore.

They're just sisters.

14.
Poetry Judge
Mark Hudson

Once, I judged a children's contest,
deciding which poem would be the best.
To find out which one I would cherish,
even though the rest might perish.
A friend gave me the responsibility.
Perhaps he was a bit too busy.
I read children's poems, a hundred or so;
all very good, but nothing like Poe.
The one I chose to be number one,
was from a kid who didn't have much fun.
His poetry told of his Hispanic dad,
who wasn't educated, which was sad.
He worked lots of manual labor;
yet couldn't keep up with wealthy neighbors.
He told his son without reservation,
"You simply must get an education."
So the young Hispanic child wrote a poem,
about studying hard while still at home,
so he could grow up and be a success,
and unlike his dad, he'd have less of stress.
This was the poem I liked the most;
a child who had pride but didn't boast.
I hope my opinion was strongly considered,
and the poem didn't end up in a pile of litter.
It's not that the other poems weren't good,
but rich kids claim they're misunderstood.
I think the truth is they're really bored.
Their parents should cut the umbilical cord.
Poor kids are detached from their parents too soon,

rich kids eat off a silver spoon.
So who really cares about the people who hurt?
"Let them eat cake-," it's their final dessert.
The government doesn't seem to care at all;
they're too busy having a ball.
So to the kid I voted for his poem to win-,
It still won't change the mess that we're in.

15.
Puzwuk The Orphan Boy And
The Starving Time
Edward Ahern

This is a retelling of and homage to a tale from Told Beneath the Northern Lights by Roy J. Snell (Little, Brown and Company 1925). The word Eskimo has been replaced with the native American name for the same reason that I'd prefer to be called Irish-American rather than Mick or Bog Trotter.

Some while ago, in the now Alaskan place where the mountains came down to the sea, and in spring the walrus swam close to shore, and a man could cross the narrow ocean in a skin boat, was the Yapik village of Kingegan. In the village lived Teragloona, an old-man teller of stories.

When the winter snow swept unhindered down the beach, and no hunters went in or out of the lodge, when the seal oil lamps burnt yellow and red, Teragloona would sit cross legged on the bed ledge and tell stories.

"Ubagok canok," he would say. "Here is something I am telling you."

He sat mending his net by the light of a seal oil lamp. "Many times in the not-so-long-ago there was no food. In one of these times, the wind had blown the ice hard on shore, so there were no seals. The walrus had gone south and the white bear did not come. There were no birds in the hills, no fish in the sea. Men went to the meat shelf and came back saying, 'cowcow peeluck'- no food.

"The villagers sat by their oil lamps and began to starve. There was little seal oil, and as the lamps went out, one by one, death threatened in the starving time of not-so-long-ago. In that time there was an orphan boy named Puzwuk." Old Teragloona had been speaking slowly, and he began speaking slower still. "He was not like other boys, that Puzwuk. His mother had died of sickness and his father had been carried off on an ice floe. He was passed from family to family, but no one accepted him for long, for he was too young to work, but ate as much as anyone else. Sometimes he was able to sleep on skins and eat pickled seal heart, but most times he slept on dirt and munched gristly polar bear necks.

"Finally a widow took him in and cared for him alongside her own son. And Puzwuk, to make himself stronger, began to run. At first he ran up and down the beach, then up and down the hills behind the village. He became the fastest, strongest runner in the village, with lungs like barrels and legs of iron. And then came this starving time.

"There were no seals to be caught, and the walrus had gone south. The polar bears did not come down from the north- there were no fishes, no birds, and no foxes. It was the starving time. As the oil lamps went out, the cold crept in, and the villagers crowded into the cosgy, the main lodge.

"Only Puzwuk was strong enough to still go hunting each day. The other villagers only huddled together and cried 'El-lect-pon-a-muck'- this is entirely too bad. Puzwuk went out every day, finding nothing and was about to give up, when one day he saw little dark spots on the snow. The spots were tiny birds, sand pipers.

"Puzwuk ran so fast he was able to grab one of the sandpipers. When he brought the bird to the cosgy that night the villagers cried, 'See, see. He has a bird. How foolish we were to put him out of our house.' But a sandpiper has meat only the size of a thumb, and each of the villagers was able to only get the hint of a taste.

"The next day Puzwuk was able to catch two sandpipers, the day after that three. But the tiny birds could not provide enough meat, and the villagers continued to weaken.

"When Puzwuk went out again to hunt, he ran up into the hills. There his sharp eyes could see ptarmigans, little birds the size of quail. Ptarmigan feathers are all white, and the birds had hidden their black bills in the snow, but Puzwuk saw them anyway. And even though they flushed and started to fly away he was able to run down one of the birds and bring it back to the village.

"'Oh! See!' The villagers yelled out. 'He has a ptarmigan. How sorry we are that we put the boy out of our house.' The villagers each ate a small, small bit of the bird, but were still too weak to move about, and so the next day Puzwuk once more set out to hunt alone. As with the sandpipers, each day Puzwuk was able to catch one more bird. But it was not enough. More seal oil lamps sputtered out, and the villagers grew colder and weaker. On the fourth day of running up into the hills Puzwuk happened to look back and saw a mist rising from the ice far out to sea. As he stared he saw the mist rise high, then disappear, and then rise again. 'Ahneca,' he thought. 'There is open water out there, and there are seals in the open water. The mist is their breath. When it disappears they have dived, and when the mist reappears the seals have surfaced. I am too far away today, but tomorrow I will hunt for seal.'

"When he awoke the next morning the cosgy was completely black, not a single oil lamp burning. 'Now it will become cold, very cold,' he said. And when Puzwuk looked in the villagers' eyes he saw that the light had died there as well, that they did not move, and scarcely breathed. 'They are starved and perhaps will freeze,' he thought. But he remembered the rising mist. 'Perhaps,' he told the villagers, 'I may get a seal today.'

"It was a long trudge from the village to the spot of open water. The ice had heaped in great jagged piles. The boy moved slowly and carefully but even so, fell often on the slick ice, banging his arms and legs on the sharp fragments. At last he came to the open pool. 'Ahneca,' he whispered to himself. 'There are seals here.'

"Puzwuk crept up to the water's edge and waited patiently for two hours until a young seal surfaced in range of his harpoon. He speared the seal and dragged it out of the water. He began singing happily, 'I-I-am-ah' and the falls and bruises on the walk back to the village seemed not to hurt. He threw open the flap to the cosgy and dragged in the seal, 'See what I have,' he yelled.

" 'Oh! See!' cried out the starving ones. 'He has a seal. How foolish we were to put the boy out of our house.' The widow had enough strength to cut up the seal and give each villager a thin slice of meat and a strip of blubber. The villagers grumbled, saying that each should have had bigger slices, but felt better and thanked the boy.

"Then Puzwuk gathered twigs together and made a fire, hanging a strip of blubber above it. Soon one seal oil lamp was glowing red and yellow, then two, then five. And the villagers began to hope that, after all, they might not starve and freeze.

"The next day the boy went back to the open water and was able to spear two seals, then strained and panted until he had dragged the two seals back to his village. And the next day, again, he harpooned a seal.

"But on the fourth day, after harpooning two seals, Puzwuk was caught in a raging blizzard that blew the snow like a pelt over him. The boy lost his way, and was afraid he would freeze in the howling storm. But he did not give up, and dragged the two seals after him. Finally he came to a shore. He knew that this was not his shore, but could see a faint light, and hoped to find shelter in a house. When he entered the house he saw several thin people huddled around a lone oil lamp, which flicked with its last drops of oil.

" 'This is too bad,' Puzwuk said, 'You have no food. But see, even though this is not a proper visit, you may have my two seals.' They took his gift gratefully and prepared meat and rendered seal oil for the lamps. When the storm had blown over Puzwuk left and after two days had found his way home. He told the widow what he had done. She was not angry.

" 'What you have done is good,' she said. 'Always do that way and you will never lack game to hunt.'

Teragloona stopped telling the story long enough to shift the seal net in his lap so he could work on a new spot. "The next morning, Puzwuk took down his harpoon and walked back out to the open water to hunt for seal. But there were no seals at the hole in the ice and Puzwuk decided he must walk further out and find another spot.

"He walked further out, where the ice was drifting and piling up, and where giant icebergs had gone aground. Puzwuk was walking around the base of a huge iceberg when he heard a loud, coarse roar. He thought the sound came from another iceberg breaking apart and falling into the water, and continued walking. But the roar came again, louder and fiercer.

"Puzwuk stopped and turned, holding his breath, trying to see the source of the roar. Then, Ahneca! A huge white bear came snuffling around the edge of the iceberg. Matna! Such a bear he was, with powerful forepaws, thick neck, gleaming eyes and bright teeth.

"The bear never paused, for this was his starving time as well. He roared even louder and charged, hoping to crack the boy's bones with his ivory teeth. 'Ahneca! Matna!,' yelled the boy, and began to run around the base of the iceberg, with the bear chasing after him. Bears can run faster than man, but Puzwuk was able to hold his distance as they circled around and around the ice.

"Puzwuk heard the bear's hoarse breathing coming closer, and willed his legs to move faster. All this while the boy had held onto his harpoon, and he had a desperate idea. 'There is a spot of soft ice on the side of this iceberg,' he thought. ' Each time I pass it I will give it a hard jab with my harpoon. When the space is big enough I can crouch inside it.'

"And so he did, running round and around the ice, jabbing each time until there was a big enough space for him to hide in. Puzwuk ran even faster, putting more distance between him and the bear, then jumped into the recess, turned around, and prepared to strike.

" 'I may be killed,' Puzwuk thought, 'but the meat we could eat and the bone marrow we could suck from this bear would keep us from starving until spring.' The boy heard the rasping breathing approach, and when he saw the bear's breath mist in front of him he struck. The harpoon entered just behind the bear's front shoulder blade and pierced its heart. The bear dropped with a roar and skidded many feet down the ice. It was dead.

"Puzwuk returned to the village and told his people of the bear. 'Those of you who are strong enough,' he said, 'come with me so we can bring back the meat, bones and pelt. There will be plenty for all."

Teragloona put down his net and stared at those in the lodge before speaking again. "There was plenty, and the starving time passed. Little Puzwuk, unwanted except for a poor widow, had saved his village. Tiny sandpipers, little ptarmigan, seals and a great white bear, he found and killed them all. But think, had he not started with one tiny sandpiper, all in the village would have died."

16.
Ripple Effect
Janis Butler Holm

As a little girl reading fairy tales, I came across the word "replied." Though a bookish child, I somehow read "replied" as "rippled," as in

"Because I said so," the prince rippled. It seemed to me that a handsome prince would speak in a breezy manner; his language would roll trippingly off the tongue. Even as a child, I understood that royalty can be casual about things the rest of us take seriously.

"I've slain the dragon," the prince rippled.

"I'll wake her with a kiss," the prince rippled.

"You will be my queen," the prince rippled.

"Of course I have a mistress," the prince rippled.

17.
Running Home, Frightened...
Arriving Home, Crying
J. J. Steinfeld

Running home, frightened,
insults on you like spit
you need to look up words
delve into sad histories
comprehend the annals of malice

your speed is immeasurable
your pain one day to be strength
but not now
now it is speed, running,
from and toward in dispute

stride for stride you go with the past
and if you leap or fall
either way you will learn to laugh
laughter a cunning wisdom
from and toward clasp identities

you are always who you were
shuffling memories like cards
in a game with tyrants
some of them so small
you think they're children at school

arriving home, crying,
your mother is at the front door
a life of waiting for you
before you can show your new scars
she comforts you in Yiddish.

18.
Snake In The Hallway
Kerry E.B. Black

A displaced encounter with nature interrupted six-year-old Alexis' early morning call of nature. Her myopic eyes widened with fear. She screamed, and then reached around to bang on her biggest sister's door.

Bang, bang, bang. Bang, bang, bang. "Dylan, get up, please! Oh please! There is a snake in the hallway!"

Neglecting her spectacles, thirteen-year-old Dylan leapt from a dream to rescue her sister. "Where?"

Alexis' wavering finger pointed out the offender. "Right there, outside of the bathroom! It's a real, live snake! I just heard it hissing."

Dylan's near-sighted, sleep-addled vision swam, and she added her scream to the morning air. "RC, get up! There is a snake!" She implored her fifteen-year-old brother.

Both girls yelled, voices straining, "Please, RC, please help us!" He did not respond.

While they screamed, their handicapped sister, Sarah, crawled to see what the fuss involved. Having the advantage of superior eyesight and proximity to the floor, she looked up, confused.

The girls' pleas changed. "Get away from it, Sarah, before it bites you!" The girls gasped. "What are you doing, Sarah! Don't touch it!" Alexis cried, bouncing from leg to leg, uncertain what to do. Dylan gasped, paralyzed.

"Guys," Sarah said, "It's not a snake." She picked up the offender, a convincing bit of string with a knot at the end that, to a nearsighted pair of eyes, resembled a head, and frayed ends to represent a tongue. "It's a rope."

19.
Special Rosie
Mark Hudson

Six-year-old Rosie has brain tumors.
She treats them with a sense of humor.
She's had hundreds of medical operations;
yet she shows incredible cooperation.
Her family gains strength from her gratitude;
this blessed child with a good attitude.
She dreams of being a rock star someday;
she already is, some might say.
She sees the beauty in a dog or a flower,
even though each day could be her final hour.
Her family enjoys every moment they spend;
and to other children, she is a great friend.
Oh, if only the rest of us could somehow be
just like her-, joyous and free.
Benefits are created to honor this child,
and all the people she's helped make smile.
Rosie wouldn't mind being a chemo nurse,
because she already has been through the worst.
She has a lot of pain in her brain;
but she is an angel because she doesn't complain.

20.
The A to Z List Of My Childhood Memories
Wendy Kennar

I spent four years working in a public library and five years teaching kindergarten. Naturally, the alphabet comprised a large portion of my day for those nine years. Consequently, I now tend to look at the world and want to arrange things alphabetically. Upon reflecting on my childhood memories, I wanted to organize what could have been jumbled chaos. It's interesting to consider the moments and experiences that have stayed with me all these years later. Hence, the A to Z List of my Childhood Memories.

A Avocado for me, tomato for my sister. My mom prepared dinner salads regularly, but did customize them with our favorite vegetables.

B Barbie car. My sister and I earnestly wanted a bubble-gum-pink Barbie car. What we got was a dark gray car, that wasn't an official "Barbie" car. Our dolls still fit, and although it was loud, we loved pushing it around the floor. It was, after all, better than no car at all.

C Cake mix. Birthdays were celebrated with chocolate cake, prepared with a mix. The cake was baked within the blue and white box that was included in the package mix. There are many pictures with either my sister or I leaning over to blow out the candle that was nestled within the middle of the cake in the blue-and-white box.

D	Dinner as a family.	Not until high school, when part-time jobs got in the way, did we have regular interruptions of this tradition.	Whenever we could, we waited for my dad to come home, so we could all eat together.	Now as a parent myself, I continue the tradition in my own home.

E	End of the week dinner.	When I was in high school, we had a period of time when our family celebrated the end of the work week at the local mall.	Everyone was allowed to select their own meal from the food court establishments and after we ate together, we browsed a bit before returning home.

F	Fraser.	That is our family surname.	It is commonly misspelled.	Sometimes including a "z" and/or an "i."	And when the sitcom *Frasier* starring Kelsey Grammer aired, our name was commonly misspelled with an "s" and an "i."

G	Gatorade.	I don't remember the specifics, but I remember my dad once got sick, and then there was a lot of Gatorade in the house.	I liked the pretty colors and was allowed to try it.	I enjoyed the beverage, my favorite flavor being lemon-lime.

H	Holidays.	Because my mom was raised in an Orthodox Jewish family, and my dad was raised as a Baptist, holidays in our home were a "mash-up."	We tended to combine the best of both worlds.	Therefore, we lit a menorah and received a gift on the first night of Chanukah.	We decorated an artificial Christmas tree, hung stockings, and received multiple gifts Christmas morning.	And we commonly ate a Christmas ham with latkes.

I	Ice cream table.	That's what my mom called the small round table and two chairs that were put in the kitchen as the special table my sister and I sometimes shared.	When I moved into my first apartment, that same ice cream table would serve as my first dining table.

J   Jump rope.   One summer while in elementary school, I tried to keep track of the number of jumps I accomplished each day.   I would write them in a small book and try to tally them up.   I wanted a summer-wide count.   That endeavor proved to be difficult to accurately calculate.

K   Kisses.   There were always kisses in our childhood home.   Kisses when we went to sleep and when we woke up.   Kisses when we went to school, kisses when we returned home from school.   Kisses randomly throughout the day.

L   Lunches.   My sister and I never made our own school lunches.   They were diligently packed by my mom, often containing an "I love you" note or a little surprise, such as a chocolate chip cookie.   Some lunches were favorites (tuna sandwiches, salad with French dressing), some were not (cream cheese sandwiches, cold corn dogs).

M   Multiple pairs of socks.   During the winter, the cold seemed to permanently camp out within our home.   It would take multiple pairs of socks for me to get warm enough to sleep at night.   Not until I moved out, did I realize that most people's homes weren't that cold; we just had a poor heating system.

N   Night time ritual.   When my sister and I would kiss our dad good-night, he always pressed down on the tops of our heads.   His rationale: he wanted us to stop growing up so fast.

O   Odd Box.   My sister and I loved to play store.   We had a small adding machine that even printed out a receipt.   And we made our own credit card for our store, which we named "The Odd Box."

P   Purple.   During pre-school, my sister went through a phase when she wouldn't leave the house without wearing something purple, her favorite color. Pants, a shirt, a barrette, socks, or a bracelet would suffice.

Q   Question. We were encouraged to question our parents and to voice our opinions -- all done respectfully, of course. Our parents were always willing to listen to our point of view, and even if my sister and I didn't get our way, we knew that we at least had the opportunity to be heard.

R   Reading. We were a family of readers. Each summer my mom regularly took my sister and me to the public library on a regular basis so we could participate in the summer reading program. We always wanted to read as many books as we could. Often, we'd start reading in the car, before we had even left the library parking lot.

S   Saturday afternoon television viewing. I remember a period of time when my sister and I were granted a little television marathon time. We'd watch back-to-back episodes of our favorites, including *The Facts of Life* and *Family Ties*. I always thought my mom was being so nice letting us watch television for an extended period of time, but as a parent now myself, I'm sure she welcomed the break it gave her.

T   Tickling. Our whole family is ticklish, and my dad loved to "get" us. He'd capture us in a big bear hug and from there, it would become a tickle-fest. Eventually, we'd call for our mom to "help us!"

U   Wake up. My sister wasn't a "morning person." Sometimes, the only thing that would rouse her from bed was my rendition of the song "Wake Up Little Susie," substituting "Susie" for "Julie."

V   Visits to malls. During summer vacation, my mom, sister, and I would frequently visit different malls. We'd have lunch in the food court, and wander from store to store (purchasing was secondary). Our favorites were, sadly, stores that aren't even in existence any more (book stores and music stores).

W   Winter pajamas. As a young girl, I spent winter sleeping in footsie pajamas. The one-piece "uniforms" (my mom's name for them) kept us warm, but I longed for spring. Spring meant two-piece pajamas, when my feet were free to feel the cool sheet.

X   Extra gifts. My mom had a "present drawer." It was where we went when we needed a last minute gift. In the event that we were just made aware of a teacher's birthday, we were able to acknowledge the occasion with a gift.

Y   Yours and mine. My sister and I spent our childhood sharing a bedroom. As we got older, we seemed to get more assertive and more territorial regarding things that were "yours" and "mine."

Z   Zebras are white with black stripes. I learned that on a "Daddy-Daughter-Date." My dad and I ventured from Los Angeles to San Diego, to spend a few days at the Wild Animal Park, the Zoo, and Sea World. We did take close-to-home family trips, but these "dates" were something special just for my dad and me.

21.
The Green Blanket
Melissa Grunow

The hand-me-down sandals I was about to strap to my feet still fit my cousin better than they fit me, but it was either next summer's sandals or last fall's tennis shoes, so I opted for the sandals.

I was sitting on the brown carpet in our small living room. I scooted forward as I reached for the first shoe, feeling my legs get warm from the friction. The sandal didn't look brand new, but the straps were in good shape and the bottoms hadn't been completely worn out. As I bent forward to buckle them, my long, red ponytail dangled over my left shoulder. Sweat appeared on my forehead, and I used the back of my hand to wipe it off. It was already a hot day, and I hadn't even eaten lunch yet.

I was six the summer it refused to rain and everything outside was as brown as the mobile home I lived in with my parents and my younger brother. Typically, I didn't even wear shoes when I was playing outside, but the dead grass felt like needles pressing into the soles of my feet. So I decided to dig through my closet until I found the sandals that I wasn't supposed to wear until the next year.

After I finished buckling my left sandal (which was always the hardest for me), I stood up and shook my feet, testing my buckling job, trying to determine how fast I could run down the street without tripping. I would have to be careful or not run at all.

I wandered into the kitchen to get some milk before going outside. The tired vacuum cleaner buzzed in the back bedroom, so I knew Mom was awake and already on one of her cleaning sprees. She cleaned every day. Once she spent the entire day taking all the dishes out of the cupboard, washing the dishes and the cupboards, then putting everything back in. She has also spent a whole day scrubbing the walls and the ceilings, ironing and reorganizing everything in my dad's closet, shampooing the carpets (I had to stay outside until they dried and had to use a neighbor's bathroom), and scrubbing the tile floors.

Mom came into the kitchen just as I was rinsing my glass and setting it in the sink.

I jumped a little when I saw her. "Can I go play outside?"

She just stood there with her arms folded across her chest. "Where are you going?"

"To Chrissy, Clifford, and Amber's. We wanna build forts."

Mom was quiet for a minute as she just stared at me. Her long hair was frizzy and stuck to her face in all kinds of places. She wore sweat pants and a tank top and her feet were bare. Her toes had flecks of red polish on them, and they were already starting to look wrinkled. And even at twenty-five, so was her face.

"Why do you have those on your feet?" She pointed at the sandals.

I shrugged.

"You're not supposed to wear them until next summer. They're too big!"

"My other shoes are too small. They hurt my feet." I hid one foot behind my calf, hoping she would change her mind.

"You're going to ruin those before you're even supposed to wear them." She pointed to the bedroom door. "Take them off and get outside."

I knew better than to argue with her. I walked slowly to my room, sat down on the floor and began unbuckling. They were hard to put on and take off because the straps were kind of thick and the latch didn't fit right in the hole. After I wiggled my feet free, I tossed them into the closet, skipped through the living room, and let the screen door slam shut behind me.

"Can the kids come out?" I yelled as I banged on their screen door. Chrissy and our friend Kathleen came to the door, each with a pink Barbie bag loaded with all kinds of stuff to help us build our forts.

"Let's go to your house," Chrissy said to me. "You have the most chairs."

Amber emerged with a big blanket rolled into a tight ball.

"The green blanket!" Kathleen said. "It always makes the best forts."

We walked back to my yard, and threw everything down in the grass. I opened the shed behind the trailer so we could each grab lawn chairs, a sleeping bag with a broken zipper, and my old picnic table. When I was three, I got the blue Smurf table for Christmas which was perfect for hosting tea parties. When I got too big to sit at it, we flipped it over and used it as a teeter-totter until the plastic started to crack.

"Hey what about those?" Amber asked, pointing to two wood things that my dad used to cut stuff. He called them horses.

"We can use those," I said with a big grin. Amber and I dragged them back to the rest of the stuff. My feet were starting to hurt from walking on the grass and the hot concrete, but I didn't say anything. I was too excited about our project.

That day, we constructed the best fort we had ever built. Kathleen and Chrissy got more blankets while Amber and I built the frame; the horses were staggered to create a hallway, and we got two other rooms built, too. The last thing we did was throw the green blanket over the top to make the roof.

After we finished tucking the blankets just right, weighing down the chairs so they wouldn't tip over and setting everything up, we were ready to crawl inside.

It was much cooler in the fort than it was outside, so we played in it all day. Kathleen's mom brought us chocolate chip cookies after lunch and we pretended we were a royal family living in a castle big enough to fill an island.

Sitting in one of the rooms, I looked at all the shadows cast on the other blankets from the sun shining through the green blanket. Whenever we used that blanket to build forts, I forgot that I wasn't wearing shoes, and that I was hungry because Mom was too busy cleaning to feed me, and that I would probably get spanked for something that night. I forgot all those things, and only thought about how nice and cool and safe I felt in that fort that was held together by the green blanket.

As the sun started to dim that day, my friends packed up their toys to go home which meant the fort had to come apart, too. We slowly dismantled it, each of us taking our own pieces home with us. I made sure to fold the green blanket so Amber could carry it, making sure none of the edges would drag on the ground as she walked to the end of the block, her sandals slapping against the bottom of her heels.

22.
The Memory Of A Baseball Fan
J. J. Steinfeld

When my closest friend's grandfather went crazy
during the 1960 Fall Classic, third game,
for the next game's pre-game show
he invited all his friends to visit
and listen to the small man's outpourings;
there on the sofa he lay
closed eyes to the ceiling, thoughts to the past,
a Yiddish-accented commentator
his voice soft as clouds above a forgotten stadium
his breath pushing away memory's displeasure:
he named all the 1950 Brooklyn Dodgers
every significant stat and score, standings from that year,
and like a Biblical scholar gone rapturous
described Robinson sliding into second
Reese scooping up a grounder
and flipping the ball to Hodges
Snider hitting a home run
Newcombe striking out another batter
Furillo making a dazzling catch
Campanella throwing out a runner
highlights from a life
God listening to the game with one ear
like an ordinary baseball fan
caught up in the beauty and excitement
of a world less defective than the ordinary.

My closest friend's grandfather
fearsome in his smallness
and shouts for retrieval

born in a baseball-less shtetl in Poland
he had leapt from a painting by Chagall
if he could still leap
except with his words
like fly balls to all fields
and he could bunt
throw knuckleballs
knuckleballs that gyrated
defied gravity
danced through time.

When my closest friend's grandfather went crazy
I first glimpsed the gracefulness of memory and madness.

23.
The Play Structure
Celia P. Ransom

There I was on a Saturday morning gratefully sipping my first cup of coffee of the day, when I heard a racket coming from next door. I wondered what was happening. What was disturbing my peaceful start to the day? So out I went, coffee cup in hand, to investigate.

My neighbor Mike and his daughter Caroline were pounding away at the play structure that had been in their yard for well over ten years. The slide, swings, teeter totter—all set aside. The two of them were deconstructing the wooden framework that supported the various apparatus. Mike explained that the kids had outgrown the play structure and that it was time for it to disappear. For him and even for me, it was not without some sadness as it was just another reference to the passing of time as we watched the children grow. Not only did his children use the play structure over the years but so did the neighborhood kids and my grandchildren.

I continued to watch for a time. The canopied tower was demolished as well as the wooden ladder leading up to it. Seeing the downfall made me recall a day with my granddaughter, Cassie. She must have been close to six-years-old. I picked her up after school and went to my house. We busied ourselves with making cookies. When we were finished, she asked if she could play on the structure in the neighbor's yard. I told her that ordinarily it would be fine, but I had observed that all the neighborhood four-to-seven-year old boys were playing there. I told her that they might not want her in their territory. "You know how boys can be."

She said with great confidence—"I will be all right, Grandma."

"Okay", I said. "But—if the boys are not nice to you, come right back." Off she went. From my kitchen window, I could see her swinging and talking to the boy in the next swing. All seemed to be well. Suddenly she jumped off the swing and came running toward my house. I went to the rear door to meet her. Smiling, with her hand cupped to her mouth in a conspiratorial tone, she said, "Don't worry, Grandma. It's going great!" She turned and went back to the play structure and the boys.

I remember how amused I was by her comment but, moreover, I was impressed that she felt the need to report back to me, thinking that I might be worried about her status. How thoughtful that was.

Later that afternoon, we made dinner for Grandpa. We three ate together that evening, after which I took her home. To this day I am still bemused remembering her statement. She is thirteen now, but thinking back, I have to agree with that little six year old girl's assessment. With her around there are no worries, it's going great.

24.
The Young And The Old
Mark Hudson

On my vacation to Wisconsin, I arrive with my aging parents. My sister brings my niece and nephew the next day.

As Ashley arrives she screams, "Grandma!" and runs up and gives my mother a big hug. My mother has been battling cancer, and each year could be her last.

Ashley always prays my mom lives one more year, so she can have presents for Christmas or her birthday. On Sunday, we celebrate my niece's birthday.

I look forward to that day. But the day will come where I'll celebrate my niece's birthday, and my mother will no longer be there. My niece will be around, and in my niece I see a tiny bit of what my mother must've been like as a little girl.

Oh God, protect all these little girls and boys. Guide them safely to your house, where everybody stays young forever.

Contributing Authors

Allen Kopp

Allen Kopp

Allen Kopp lives in St. Louis, Missouri, USA.

He has over a hundred short stories appearing in such diverse publications as *The Penmen Review, Belle Reve Literary Journal, A Twist of Noir, Burial Day Books, Dew on the Kudzu: A Journal of Southern Writing, Short Story America, Offbeat Christmas Story Anthology, Skive Magazine, Creaky Door Magazine, Gothic City Press: Gas Lamp, Churn Thy Butter, Wordhaus, Fictitious Magazine, Gaia's Misfits Fantasy Anthology, Back Hair Advocate, Typehouse Magazine, Through the Gaps,* and many others.

His Internet home is: www.literaryfictions.com

Celia P. Ransom

Celia P. Ransom

Where are you from?
Except for a brief time in Texas when my husband was stationed at Fort Hood, I have lived in Michigan my whole life – a long one.

When and why did you begin writing?
I began writing poetry seven years ago, when I found myself in a position of caretaker for two family members, my husband and my mother. The writing served as a release. The stories in The Grey Wolfe Storybook 2014 are my first efforts at prose.

What would you say is your most interesting writing quirk?
In early morning in semi-sleep, words and thoughts meander through my mind and I have to get up and write them down. I then go right back to sleep.

What do you like to do when you're not writing?
I enjoy time spend with friends and family, reading and summers by Long Lake in Traverse City.

As a child what did you want to do when you grew up?
I wanted to be in the movies!

Edward Ahern

Edward Ahern

Where are you from?
Chicago; Cranston, Rhode Island; Washington, D.C.,; Bremerhaven, Germany; Yokosuka, Japan; Fairfield, Connecticut; Walton on Thames, England; Fairfield, Connecticut.

When and why did you begin writing?
On retirement, three and a half years ago. Forty-seven stories published thus far.

What would you say is your most interesting writing quirk?
I think out the entire story idea before making notes or beginning to write.

What do you like to do when you're not writing?
Fly fish, shoot sporting clays, attend German, French and Japanese conversation groups.

As a child, what did you want to do when you grew up?
Archeology.

J. J. Steinfeld

J. J. Steinfeld

Where are you from?
Prince Edward Island, Canada

When and why did you begin writing?
Probably around the age of four or five, when I became captivated by the world of imagination, and began putting some of my imaginative thoughts onto paper.

What would you say is your most interesting writing quirk?
That I sometimes turn my poems into short stories and my short stories into one-act plays.

What do you like to do when you're not writing?
Take long walks or bicycle rides... and think about what I'm going to do creatively next.

As a child, what did you want to do when you grew up?
Write stories, poems, and plays... and be a professional baseball player, especially a fastball pitcher like Sandy Koufax. The baseball goal didn't materialize... not even close.

Canadian fiction writer, poet, and playwright J. J. Steinfeld lives on Prince Edward Island, where he is patiently waiting for Godot's arrival and a phone call from Kafka. While waiting, he has published fourteen books, including *Disturbing Identities* (Stories, Ekstasis Editions), *Anton Chekhov Was Never in Charlottetown* (Stories, Gaspereau Press), *Would You Hide Me?* (Stories, Gaspereau Press), *An Affection for Precipices* (Poetry, Serengeti Press), *Misshapenness* (Poetry, Ekstasis Editions), and *A Glass Shard and Memory* (Stories, Recliner Books). His short stories and poems have appeared in numerous periodicals and anthologies internationally, and over forty of his one-act plays and a handful of full-length plays have been performed in Canada and the United States.

Janel Mills

Janel Mills

Where are you from?
Wayne, Michigan.

When and why did you begin writing?
I began writing regularly about five years ago, when I realized writing was a more constructive way to cope with my feelings towards motherhood than eating large amounts of junk food.

What would you say is your most interesting writing quirk?
I swear a lot more in my writing than I do in real life. When editing my work, I often find myself asking, "Do I really need an f-word there, or would it be more effective there?"

What do you like to do when you're not writing?
When I'm not writing, I'm either working at my day job as a librarian, making my kids take a bath, or watching whatever TV series I'm currently obsessed with on Netflix.

As a child, what did you want to do when you grew up?
When I was a child, I wanted to be a veterinarian. My first college chemistry class forced me to reconsider this career path.

Janis Butler Holm

Janis Butler Holm

Where are you from?
Originally: Houston, Texas.

When and why did you begin writing?
First grade. Learning to write was mandatory.

What would you say is your most interesting writing quirk?
Brevity.

What do you like to do when you're not writing?
Dinner with friends.

As a child, what did you want to do when you grew up?
Magazine journalism.

Jon Moray

Where are you from?
I am from Kissimmee, Florida

When and why did you begin writing?
I began writing over four years ago because I felt I had good story ideas that should be read and not kept only to my imagination.

What would you say is your most interesting writing quirk?
My most interesting writing quirk is my desire to include a surprise twist ending, although most of my stories written do not.

What do you like to do when you're not writing?
I enjoy my time with my family, playing basketball and training for marathons.

As a child, what did you want to do when you grew up? As a child I wanted to be a professional baseball player. The only problem was I couldn't hit, field or throw that well.

Kerry E.B. Black

Kerry E.B. Black

Where are you from?
I hail from a little suburb of Pittsburgh, Pennsylvania.

When and why did you begin writing?
Writing is an escape and a comfort. It provides me a voice when I feel mute, a tune when I need bravery. I've written since childhood and enjoy playing with words.

What would you say is your most interesting writing quirk?
As a busy parent of five children, it is not unusual to have a child swinging from my leg as I type on my laptop. I write daily, despite distractions.

What do you like to do when you're not writing?
I enjoy travelling, spending time with family and friends, taking in a good show, and of course reading; Tae Kwon Do, horsemanship, fencing, archery, and enjoying excellent cuisine.

As a child, what did you want to do when you grew up?
I wanted to be a jockey, spent hours training, but then a growth spurt stole that dream.

Mark Hudson

Mark Hudson

Where are you from?
Evanston, Illinois.

When and why did you begin writing?
I went to Columbia College in Chicago to study animation, because I'm an artist, but found it complicated, so I switched my major to fiction writing. I'm better at writing poetry than fiction, but do write stories when they come to me.

What would you say is your most interesting writing quirk?
My most interesting writing quirk is I don't know what a quirk is. And you can print that. Might as well add a little humor

What do you like to do when you're not writing?
I also draw, taking an art class at Noyes art center and a private portraiture class.

As a child, what did you want to do when you grew up?
My first goal was to be a garbage man. But then I didn't do well in high school, and ended up with a lot of jobs dealing with taking out trash. Many artists I know had mundane jobs before they got their art education, and you appreciate being able to write and do art when you've had lousy jobs.

Melissa Grunow

Melissa Grunow

Where are you from?
I was born in Saginaw, but I grew up in Oak Park. I now live in Ferndale.

When and why did you begin writing?
I was always an avid reader as a child, so the interest in stories naturally evolved to writing. I started writing regularly in middle school—thriller short stories with predictable plot twists and angst-filled poetry—that were terrible and a little embarrassing. We all have to start somewhere, though, and that was my beginning. Eventually my writing matured as I matured, and I found my writing voice in college and thereafter, as I began publishing creative nonfiction and short stories.

What would you say is your most interesting writing quirk?
I get a lot of my writing ideas while I'm driving, so I carry a digital voice recorder so I can capture my ideas before they leave my mind.

What do you like to do when you're not writing?
I'm a full-time college English instructor, so I spend a lot of time talking about writing and responding to my students' writing. I have a three-year-old husky named Duke who I love to take for long walks or to the dog park in Detroit. I read a lot, too. I don't watch much television, though I enjoy watching reruns of Friends and Criminal Minds or relaxing with my boyfriend while we enjoy a Netflix marathon.

As a child, what did you want to do when you grew up?
I went through the experience of wanting to be an astronaut, a police officer, a doctor. None of those future professions stuck with me like writing. I always hoped to be a writer, even though I didn't write anything creative for almost the entire decade of my twenties. Luckily, writing and I found each other again about three years ago, and I started publishing my work around that time as well.

My publications and information about my work can be found at www.melissagrunow.com and you can find me on Twitter at @mel_the_writer.

Melodie Corrigal

Melodie Corrigal

Where are you from?
Vancouver, British Columbia, Canada.

When and why did you begin writing?
Started at age ten to escape the chaos of my family to a more interesting world where I called the shots.

What would you say is your most interesting writing quirk?
Am very eclectic writer. Have tried everything from literary efforts to whimsy.

What do you like to do when you're not writing?
Reading, going to theatre, travelling and playing with my grandchildren.

As a child, what did you want to do when you grew up?
Like my husband, my career aspirations were to be a pirate.

Robert McGuill

Robert McGuill

Where are you from?
Colorado – by way of Wisconsin, Maryland, Kansas, Illinois and
Iowa.

When and why did you begin writing?
Right out of college.   I was hired by an agency to write promotional
copy, and it's what I've done my whole career.   I began writing
fiction about ten years ago; an experiment in self-enrichment.

What would you say is your most interesting writing quirk?
I often compose one-handed, owning the cats who insist on making
my keyboard their bed

What do you like to do when you're not writing?
Reading, fly fishing, spending time in the mountains.

As a child, what did you want to do when you grew up?
Become a secret agent.

Terry Sanville

Terry Sanville

Where are you from?
I live in the City of San Luis Obispo, on California's Central Coast, halfway between Los Angeles and San Francisco.

When and why did you begin writing?
In 1974 I began work as a city planner, writing technical reports (5-10K words per day). After retiring in 2003, I pursued a life-long dream of writing fiction. I've always been a storyteller, and short fiction is my favorite form.

What would you say is your most interesting writing quirk?
I often start writing after the late-night TV shows go off the air, when I can sit in my bathrobe and mutter dialog lines to myself.

What do you like to do when you're not writing?
I'm also a musician, having played guitar for over fifty years (yikes! I'm that old??). I play instrumental music and perform in public at monthly events. I also help my artist/poet laureate wife with her work.

As a child, what did you want to do when you grew up?
I wanted to be an architect – like George Costanza in the old *Seinfeld* show. I liked building things. But I ended up being a city planner specializing in transportation. Close enough for jazz.

Wendy Kennar

Wendy Kennar

Where are you from?
I am a Los Angeles native and have, in fact, spent my entire life living within the same zip code.

When and why did you begin writing?
I've written since second grade, when Mrs. Jones made me a "book" with yellow construction paper cover. I write because I'm always thinking and observing, and I need to get my thoughts down. I write to organize ideas, to share, and to attempt to make sense of the world around me.

What would you say is your most interesting writing quirk?
I print out my rough drafts on scratch paper. I re-use notes from my son's school and random mailings in an effort to save paper. I also tend to get many ideas while in the shower.

What do you like to do when you're not writing?
I am an avid reader. I enjoy sitting on my patio, being near the ocean, and I love spending time with my husband and six-year-old son.

As a child, what did you want to do when you grew up?
I had hoped to become an astronaut. I memorized facts about the U.S. Manned Space Program. Then in high school, I volunteered in an elementary school classroom and decided I wanted to be a teacher. I enjoyed a twelve-year teaching career.

My blog can be found at wendykennar.blogspot.com

William Doreski

William Doreski

Where are you from?
Currently live in Peterborough, New Hampshire.   Grew up in Connecticut, lived in Boston and other places.

When and why did you begin writing?
Began in high school—attempted to prove anyone could write as well as e.e. cummings. Proved myself wrong.

What would you say is your most interesting writing quirk?
Need a cat in the room.

What do you like to do when you're not writing?
Read, hike, bicycle, drink coffee, garden, browse in the library, etc.

As a child, what did you want to do when you grew up?
I wanted to befriend a bobcat and write a book about it.

The Michigan Elks Major Project

The Michigan Elks Association assists handicapped children under the age of eighteen. The Major Project provides facilitating services essential to treatment such as special examinations, therapy and special prescriptions.

The Major Project also sponsors attendance at Speech Camps, Diabetic Camps, and Special Therapy Camps. The overall aim of the Michigan Elks Major Project is to help handicapped children become self-sufficient, healthy, contributing citizens of our communities.

The proceeds of this book are being allocated through the leadership of the Farmington Elks Lodge #1986.
30898 West Ten Mile Road
Farmington Hills, MI 48336-2606
248-476-1986
Elks1986@yahoo.com
http://web.me.com/elks_1986

Lodge Officers:
Exalted Ruler: Gregory Larscheidt
Leading Knight: Patricia McKenna
Secretary: Earl W. Wolfe (PER)